Charles Reynolds Brown

Two Parables

Charles Reynolds Brown

Two Parables

ISBN/EAN: 9783744797351

Printed in Europe, USA, Canada, Australia, Japan

Cover: Foto ©Lupo / pixelio.de

More available books at **www.hansebooks.com**

TWO PARABLES

BY
CHARLES R. BROWN
PASTOR OF THE FIRST CONGREGATIONAL CHURCH
OAKLAND, CALIFORNIA

"And without a parable spake He not unto them"

CHICAGO   NEW YORK   TORONTO
FLEMING H. REVELL COMPANY
1898

TO
MY FIRST AND BEST TEACHER
IN THOSE PLAIN TRUTHS WE LIVE BY
MY. MOTHER

Preface

This little book is not an attempt at the systematic exposition of the "Two Parables,"—that work has already been well done. It contains a series of sermons growing out of those two passages in the teachings of our Lord, and its purpose is to interpret His words and apply their lessons to the needs of common life. These sermons were preached, not consecutively, to the people of the First Congregational Church in Oakland, California, and the kindly comments of those good friends, and their oft-expressed wish to have them in permanent form, furnish me my chief reason for putting them in print.

I confess, also, to another motive. By the pressure of that more than Athenian craze to hear ever some new thing, some of us are impelled to search out the queer and odd texts that lie in the corners of holy writ. The cleverness displayed in some of the

Preface

startling selections is remarkable, but wholesome good taste often suffers in the house of those who should be its staunchest friends. "Old friends are the best;" and so are old texts. Those verses from the Bible which have passed into such common use as to form part of the circulating medium of daily speech, will, when interpreted in fresh and vital fashion, prove the most useful texts to be had. If these sermons on two of the most familiar passages in the New Testament should serve, however imperfectly, to illustrate this fact, I should count it a privilege to modestly offer them "for the good of the Order."

CHARLES R. BROWN.

Oakland, California,
    March 15, 1898.

CONTENTS

PART I

I A Definition of the word "Neighbor" 13
"Who is my neighbor? And Jesus answering said, A certain man, etc."

II The Men who Look On - - 37
"And likewise a Levite, when he was at the place came and looked on him, and passed by on the other side."

III The Man on Horseback - - 62
"But a certain Samaritan . . . went to him and bound up his wounds . . . and set him upon his own beast."

IV Unto the End - - - - 84
"Take care of him: and whatsoever thou spendest more, when I come again I will repay thee."

PART II

V The Sinful Demand for Separateness 113
"Father, give me the portion of goods that falleth to me."

VI The Hopefulness of a Sense of Need 134
"And he began to be in want."

VII The Wisdom of Refusal - - 156
"And no man gave unto him."

VIII The Naturalness of a Religious Life 181
"And when he came to himself, he said . . . I will arise and go to my father."

IX A Personal Confession - - - 205
"I have sinned against heaven and before thee."

X The Watchful Interest of the Father 225
"But when he was yet a great way off, his father saw him."

PART I

"And behold a certain lawyer stood up and tempted him, saying, Master, what shall I do to inherit eternal life? He said unto him, What is written in the law? How readest thou? And he answering said, Thou shalt love the Lord thy God with all thy heart and with all thy soul and with all thy strength and with all thy mind; and thy neighbor as thyself. And He said unto him, Thou hast answered right; this do and thou shalt live. But he, willing to justify himself, said unto Jesus, And who is my neighbor? And Jesus answering said, A certain man went down from Jerusalem to Jericho and fell among thieves who stripped him of his raiment, and wounded him and departed, leaving him half dead. And by chance there came down a certain priest that way; and when he saw him, he passed by on the other side. And likewise a Levite, when he was at the place, came and looked on him and passed by on the other side. But a certain Samaritan, as he journeyed, came where he was; and when he saw him, he had compassion on him, and went to him and bound up his wounds, pouring in oil and wine, and set him on his own beast and brought him to an inn and took care of him. And on the morrow when he departed he took out two pence and gave them to the host and said unto him, Take care of him; and whatsoever thou spendest more, when I come again I will repay thee. Which now of these three, thinkest thou, was neighbor unto him that fell among the thieves? And he said, He that shewed mercy on him. Then said Jesus unto him, Go and do thou likewise."

A Definition of the Word "Neighbor"

"Who is my neighbor? And Jesus answering said, A certain man," etc.

The lawyer came to inquire the way to inherit eternal life. Jesus threw him back upon himself. "Give your own idea of it. What is written in the law? How readest thou?" He answering said, "Thou shalt love the Lord thy God with all thy heart and with all thy soul and with all thy strength and with all thy mind; and thy neighbor as thyself." He answered right; he was thoroughly sound in that confession of faith and in his statement of the ethics of religion. He was then told to do this and he would live. But, wishing to justify himself, he demands a definition of the word "neighbor." He feels, perchance, that when the scope of the second great commandment is stated by this new teacher from

Galilee, he may still find himself well within the lines; and that in any event the reply of Jesus will afford him fresh material for comment and criticism.

You know that lawyer. He is not always a member of the bar. Sometimes he is a merchant or a mechanic, a physician—or, possibly, he may have gotten into the ministry. He is the individual who can answer right, but does not do right. He excuses his lack of performance by some quibble. He can draw you a correct plan of the way to inherit eternal life, but he worms out of it himself on some side issue. Ask him if he does not believe in being good; he will answer right, but will ask instantly what is it to be good. Ask him if it is not our duty to obey the will of God; he will answer right, and then begin to haggle with you as to what is the will of God. He will make a bold, firm statement as to one's obligation to love his neighbor, but before he lets his voice fall, he will ask, And who is my neighbor?

A Definition of the Word "Neighbor"

The text gives our Master's reply. He pointed to a certain man who went down from Jerusalem to Jericho and, falling among thieves, came to the place where he was in sore need of human help. The priest and the Levite, who saw the wounded man and passed by on the other side, were also well read in the law. They, too, could instantly have answered right, in saying that we inherit eternal life by loving God with all our powers and by loving our neighbors as ourselves. But somehow they failed to see that this applied to the case of the man who had been robbed. It would be almost fanatical to suppose that the term neighbor could be capable of such loose and careless application as to include that strange man out there among the rocks who had come to grief through no fault of theirs. However, a certain Samaritan, a heretic, who could not have answered right in all points of his theology, came along and, at great delay and with much pains, brought relief to his brother man. As Jesus paints this

Two Parables

picture, His word about neighborly love becomes flesh and dwells among us, full of grace and truth. The Samaritan was neighbor to the one who fell among the thieves. He instantly recognized in the wounded man a neighbor whom he was under obligations to love. He furnished us a full-page illustration of the meaning of the second of the two great commandments. By his own conduct, he wrote out a clear definition of that word "neighbor." Who is your neighbor? A certain man; a man near you; a man who needs you; a man whom you have it in your power to help. This parable shows us the meaning of love, and points out the neighbor to whom we are to direct that love.

The lawyer could answer right as to the words that were written in the law; he did not understand the spirit of what is written in the obligation of human brotherhood. He had not learned to interpret the law and make appropriate application to concrete cases. That was why Jesus began His

A Definition of the Word "Neighbor"

reply to him by pointing to "a certain man." Much of the enthusiasm for humanity, in our own day, is likewise mere words and cant. People use great swelling terms about their philanthropic interest and their altruistic efforts, who have not learned as yet to be neighborly with the certain men who need their service. In reality there is no "humanity" to be loved and served—nothing but certain men. There is no human need in general to be relieved, but only the wants of certain men. There is no impersonal or abstract neighbor to be loved; the only reality in the case is a certain man. The friend of the race at large is often sadly lacking in this genuine and helpful friendliness to the certain lives that stand nearest his own. So, one purpose of the reply of Jesus is to bring our love for our neighbor down out of the clouds and back out of the fog of vague generalities, and make it effective and useful by fixing it upon certain concrete men.

Two Parables

It is very easy to grow vague and gassy in religion. It is much simpler to talk grandly about great and wide enthusiasms than it is to behave lovingly toward the certain man at one's elbow. But the only love for mankind that Jesus recognizes and holds before us that we may go and do likewise, is the love that serves the wants of some certain man on life's pathway. To love your neighbor is to act the part of love toward your wife and children, toward your employer or employé, toward the streetcar conductor and the newsboy, toward all the certain men along the road who open the door of opportunity for our brotherliness. Goodness is neither a cold-blooded, shivering devotion to some abstract ideal, nor a soft indeterminate passion for ill-defined causes. It is rather faithfulness and usefulness in certain concrete social relations. It is devotion to the certain men whose need summons us to service. "A dollar given to the needy neighbor, whose worth we appreciate, whose needs we understand, whose

A Definition of the Word "Neighbor"

plans we talk over with him, whose confidence we have, is worth a hundred spent in promiscuous charity." In the latter case the man gives his check; in the former, he gives his check, plus himself.

Jesus indicated all this in the very wording of those two commandments which were to contain all the law and the prophets. Love God with all your heart, he said. That was definite. There is but one God, and no uncertainty could arise as to the heavenly side of our obligations. As to the earthly side, he did not say, "Love man;" that would have been loose and misty. There are millions of men. In the case of the overwhelming majority, it does not matter to them, practically, whether we love them or not. Our love would never become known nor effective. Loving them would be nothing more than a pleasant sentiment. The second commandment must read, Thou shalt love thy neighbor. Jesus names the certain men whom we are to love. Love some particular men who are within the length of your cabletow, and whom you have power to help.

The whole teaching of Jesus looks in that direction. The aim of conduct, as he conceived it, is not abstract saintliness, but full, rich, useful life. We are not here to spend our efforts in cultivating and nursing some deep, hidden thing called virtue; we are rather here, by God's help and grace, to cultivate, as a recent writer on ethics has said, "faithfulness and helpfulness in the actual relationships" of the family, of society, of the neighborhood, and of the church. If we do that, our virtue and our character will take care of itself. We shall have life, and have it abundantly by doing the will of God in our plain, ordinary situations. Eternal life, indeed, is knowing the true God and Jesus Christ whom He has sent. But we come to know Jesus best by serving the needs of men. Those to whom He spoke the disappointing words, "I know you not," were the foolish ones who had carelessly failed to discharge their duties in

A Definition of the Word "Neighbor"

society. Those who are commended as having been held within the loving anticipation of the Father, who from the foundation of the world was preparing a kingdom for them, are the men who helped to relieve the pain and trouble around them. Inasmuch as we have ministered unto the plain wants of men who lacked food, clothing, medicine, and friendship, we have ministered unto Him. Our whole duty, then, is comprehended in this: We must love God and we must love these certain men.

The modern plea is for close, definite, and personal relations in all forms of Christian work. The present tendency is toward charity at arm's length instead of charity at the end of a long pole, or the farther outpost of a complex organization. Charitably-inclined families are asked to know and relieve certain needy families. Unpaid, voluntary, friendly visitors, rather than officials, represent the organized relief work in many cities, and come close to the real people to be helped. The individual church still contributes to the great missionary boards, but it sometimes also sends out, under the supervision of the board, a certain man, who forms a vital bond between the foreign field and his own local church. The statement that the field is the world is thus translated from an abstract utterance of an undeniable fact into a life size picture, where we see our own flesh and blood. Our neighbor in the next pew has a daughter representing our church in India. The man who passes the plate has a son who is a medical missionary in Africa. We have a kodak picture, on the mantel at home of certain men brought from paganism into the Kingdom of God by these certain fellow Christians from our own church fireside. How much easier to really love our Buddhist neighbor, give for him and pray for him, when by this system of personal relationships he has become to us a certain man!

This definition of the word neighbor throws light, also, upon another phase of human conduct. Life is not one straight,

A Definition of the Word "Neighbor"

steady, unchanging thing. It is made up of occasions, new situations, and fresh opportunities. To be a neighborly man is to act the part of love toward the certain individual who confronts you in each situation. When the Samaritan was riding calmly along on his own beast, he was not loving that wounded traveler. He did not know there was such a man. But he rides around a bend in the road, and there is the sufferer, lying among the rocks, bleeding and half dead. Instantly the Samaritan has another neighbor whom he must love. Here is a fresh opportunity, and he meets it with devoted service. That was what Jesus meant when He told us that the neighbor whom we are to love is a certain man, providentially thrown in our way, that we may render him a kindness.

We never need to make pilgrimages to find our religious opportunities. We shall not overtake our salvation by journeying to this mountain, nor to Jerusalem, nor to any far-away situation. The man who seeks to do the will of God in spirit and in truth will find that "the place" where men ought to worship and to work is the very spot where he already stands. The Crusaders used to go to Palestine to capture the Holy Sepulchre from the Saracens. They felt they were rendering a service to Christ, and that they would find Him and His blessing there. But He was not there; He was risen. The failure of all their attempts seems like God's own rebuke upon a superstitious regard for certain soil. We do not find God by going to Palestine. He is here; He is not far from any one of us. We find Him not by a change of place, but by a change of heart. He dwells with every man who has an obedient and a contrite heart. He offers every man the completest opportunity for Christian service in the providential openings that stand along the way.

We never need to travel to find our human duties. You have seen enthusiasts rushing about to find what their hands ought to do. They tell us they are anxious to do

A Definition of the Word "Neighbor"

something for Christ, but that they do not find it. They forget that the way to serve Christ is to begin right where you are. Take certain men near you, and begin to act the part of a Christian toward them. If you are a wife, be a Christian wife. The most beautiful being on earth is a Christian wife and mother. Be a Christian husband, a Christian father, a Christian neighbor, a Christian employer, a Christian citizen. Salvation comes through faith in Christ, and when once you believe in Christ, then work your salvation out into these concrete forms of life, and God will work in you mightily to will and to do His good pleasure. There is no other Christianity than this, and the faithful fulfillment of these relations in the spirit of Christ is more than all whole burnt offerings and sacrifices.

Men who carry their heads high often overlook the real neighbors whom we are to love. We live in a day of world-wide enthusiasms and of marvelously intricate organization. We have rousing public meetings and ringing platform addresses, touching our duty to the suffering Armenians and the struggling Cubans and the starving Hindoos. We have workingmen's clubs and workinggirls' homes, missions to the masses, and missions to the slums. All these things we ought to have done, and not to leave certain other things undone. We also have a mission to the prosperous and respectable. We have great and serious obligations to certain men on our own level and in our own set. When Christian work was under the immediate direction of the Master, we read that when Andrew became a Christian, "he first findeth his own brother Simon, and saith unto him, we have found the Messiah. And he brought him to Jesus." He was trained for his broader apostleship by his fidelity to the spiritual need of the certain man who was his own brother. It was made the first duty of those Jewish Christians to see that "repentance and remission of sins should be preached in His name among all nations, *beginning at Jeru-*

A Definition of the Word "Neighbor"

salem." Even the duties which become world-wide in their extent, have their basis in the obligations we owe to the certain men who are actually in sight.

In charitable work, we must certainly employ this simple method. You think of all the hunger and cold and nakedness in the world. You wish you might relieve it all. You simply know that you cannot. It was not intended that you should. God could relieve it all, but He does not. Some of this suffering is to rebuke and correct the very sinfulness that caused it. All of it is meant for the moral education of men. You can only do your small part. You can do the work of love for certain needy men who come your way. You are not held responsible for all the want in the world. You are not even commanded to go and search it all out. The utmost command Jesus laid upon us was, "Give to every one that asketh thee." The need that in the providence of God presents itself and makes its request, you are to meet and do your best to supply. Simply, be ready! Lay aside a certain percentage of your income for benevolence. Have your heart full of love to God, and then act the part of love toward the certain men who come. Do the right deed as each separate situation opens before you. The great burden of the world's salvation, and of the world's pain, is not laid upon you alone for solution. God made the world, and God alone is at last responsible for it all. You are simply bidden to love your neighbor; and your neighbor is the certain man whose need is brought within reach of your help.

Who is my neighbor? A certain man who needs loving. A man in trouble; a man who must have neighborly help or he will die. This was the field where love was to find its adequate expression. And this love is to be no mere sentiment of the heart. The spirit of it is unseen, but it has flesh and bones. It shows its face and form in kindly actions. Loving our neighbor is doing unto him in his time of need

A Definition of the Word "Neighbor"

as the Good Samaritan did unto the certain nameless man. And our readiness to do this when the opportunity comes is the measure of our love.

Young Christians are sometimes troubled because they cannot feel more love to God and more love to man—especially to man. They covet a larger and more rosy stock of feelings. Yet, perhaps they are cultivating and maintaining all the while unselfish dispositions. They would be ready at any time to lend a hand, to make sacrifice, to go out of their way to serve a friend in need. They would wait upon the sick, or visit the stranger, or render the delicate service that is so grateful in time of sorrow. The ready willingness to do this when occasion demands, Jesus says, is loving one's neighbor. Christ did not go back along the road and ask the Samaritan about his sentiments and feelings, or cross-examine him beforehand on his brotherly attainments, to see whether he would serve as an example of neighborly love. As President Hyde well says: "The abstract self-conscious moralizing which fixes the eye of the individual on his own subjective states is the straight road to all manner of morbidness, sentimentalism, and insincerity. The healthy, ethical man fixes his eyes on objects, persons, institutions; and in doing his duty toward these, the virtues come as a matter of course." Christ waits until the Samaritan rides up to the point where he sees the traveler wounded and bloody. The way he acts then will tell the story whether or not he loves his neighbor. His conduct in the face of that demand was so exemplary that Jesus held it up, saying to the lawyer and to us all, "Go and do thou likewise."

Perhaps because I am young and have good digestion; perhaps because I have such inspiring work to do and have the peace of God in my heart, I am too much inclined to look on the bright side; but I believe there is more love and kindness in the world than we are wont to think. You will find it everywhere. You meet it in

A Definition of the Word "Neighbor"

the streets and alleys and courts all over the city. You see beautiful instances of it among those who are called poor because they have little money, but who are often rich in neighborly love. Many of these people in the humbler walks of life would fail sadly in making an address about "a love for humanity." They might cut an ill figure in prayer-meeting if they were called up to speak on the duty of loving one's neighbor, but they both know and have the spirit of it. The way that hard-working husbands and wives bear with each other, take care of each other in time of sickness, make sacrifices together for the sake of their children, doing it cheerfully as a matter of course, does great credit to this human nature of ours. The neighbors among the poor are ready for friendly service in the hour of adversity, in time of trouble and trial. When the occasion comes, they go in gladly and do their best. The woman nurses her next-door neighbor in her illness; washes up the kitchen floor, gets the children off to school, and sets a bite of supper for the husband when he returns from work, hungry, anxious and weary. All this is commonplace, but it is neighborly love of the Samaritan sort. It was what Jesus pointed out as tending toward eternal life.

You hear men sneer sometimes at human nature. "There is a great deal of human nature left in him," they say; as if human nature was always something weak and mean. Such talk is cheap and false. Human nature is not perfect, but it is the noblest thing we have here on this earth. Human goodness has its limitations, but it is the best thing current. All around us plain people are rising to great heights of self-sacrifice and making no commotion about it. Parents are working and economizing to keep their children fed, clothed and in school, seeking to make life easier for the coming generation than it was for their own. Young men and young women, even boys and girls, are working day after day, and uncomplainingly turning in their wages

A Definition of the Word "Neighbor"

to support the family. Young people are denying themselves the advantages of higher education, denying themselves love, and marriage, and homes of their own, that they may stay by the old home and use their earnings to support invalid parents or invalid sisters. What is all this unselfish love and service but an embodiment of the spirit of Christ's holy religion? They recognize these neighborly obligations, and they bravely meet them as the Samaritan met the wants of the wounded traveler. In this way they are preparing themselves to inherit eternal life.

This is certainly the way to find heaven; it is the way to develop good character, and it is the way, also, to attain present happiness. If you sit down, loving yourself, thinking about yourself, you will grow miserable. The things that belong to our deep and lasting peace are not to be found by directing our attention within nor by examination of our own attainments. Chauncey Depew stated that he had known intimately every President of the United States for the last thirty years, and every man eminent in politics, in literature or in art; and that he had never known one who was contented even with his unusual success. We are never satisfied with what we have or what we are. God did not mean that we should be. And if you should turn to the big world, and think how much wickedness and suffering and trouble there is, which you cannot change nor cure, you may simply go mad over it. As you dwell upon it, it will come to haunt you. You will find the way of healthy and useful life by doing kind deeds, by speaking kind words, and by making yourself a helpful man to the certain men whose needs come your way. And then, as to the remainder, "rest in the Lord, and wait patiently for Him." He that thus "dwelleth in love, dwelleth in God and God in him; for God is love." He that abides in the practice of such loving deeds will come to share in God's own eternal peace.

A Definition of the Word "Neighbor"

Men need two great facts to help them to live right. They need to know that God loves them, and that certain men, neighbor men and near men, love them. Life is hard for the best of us. If it is not now, it will be. Men need all the love, sympathy and help you can give them. It will become to them more than the proffer of human friendship; it will aid in preparing them to believe in and to accept the divine love. We rightly call God "Our Father." And men will be made ready to believe in and to trust Our Father just in proportion as they come to know the love and goodness of His children. The gracious compassion of that God whom no man hath seen at any time must be revealed through the mediation of consecrated flesh and blood. Jesus was the complete and perfect Son, so that He could say boldly, "He that hath seen me, hath seen the Father." But in the daily conduct of all the sons and daughters of the Most High, the world should see unmistakable indications that God the

Two Parables

Father is indeed full of grace and truth. May He, by His sufficient help, enable us to make our due contribution to these effective evidences of Christianity, through the helpful love we bear the certain men who are our neighbors!

The Men who Look On

"A Levite, when he was at the place, came and looked on him and passed by on the other side."

Men are judged by the way they conduct themselves in the face of certain openings. The whole idea of moral character rests upon the possibility of making choice. A saloon door opens before two men; one goes in, the other stays out. A church door opens; one enters, the other turns away. The door to honorable success opens; one, by industry, prudence and persistent effort, enters; the other, by careless indifference or laziness, stays out. Jesus once made a more searching statement as to the requirements of the new life, and uttered a richer promise as to how He would supply its needs. The idea of making such personal appropriation of the Christlife as to warrant him in saying, "Ye eat the flesh of the Son of Man and drink His blood," set before His hearers an open door into the deeper experiences of Christian life, but it divided them. To some it was a hard saying, and "from that time many of His disciples went back and walked no more with Him." To others, those were gracious words that proceeded out of His mouth, and these disciples came more closely to Him, saying, "To whom should we go? Thou hast the words of eternal life. And we believe and are sure that Thou art that Christ, the Son of the living God." In every case, you know the man by the way he treats his opportunity.

The same thing holds true in the parable. The wounded traveler was lying there on the roadside, needing help. He was an open door, by which any passerby could enter into noble Christian service. There came down a certain priest that way. He saw the man's need and passed by on the other side, scarcely giving it a thought.

The Men who Look On

A Levite came along, saw this door of opportunity, came over and looked in, but did not go in, and then passed by on the other side. The Samaritan alone saw the door and entered into an effective service of the wounded man, and entered at the same time into our everlasting remembrance, and into a long career of usefulness wherever kindness is practiced or preached. But this morning I want to speak to you of the Levite who looked on.

You can see him standing there on the Jericho road. He was not quite so brutally cold as the priest. He would have hotly condemned a man who passed on without a glance of pity for such distress. He came and looked down upon the suffering traveler. He inquired his name, perhaps. How many robbers were there? How much of your money did they get? Are you suffering much pain from those ugly wounds in your head? It is outrageous that the Roman Government does not ferret out the highwaymen that lurk in these rocks! Then, having gotten all the particulars so that he could relate them to his Jericho friends that night, and having expressed his great regret that such things were permitted in this wicked world, he passed by on the other side.

You have met this man, too. He is not always a Levite. Sometimes he is an American, a Californian, and he may live on our side of the bay. Sometimes he is a woman, almost out of breath over what she calls her interest in charity work. He represents the people who love to take up problems and look at them. Whenever human suffering is named, they can instantly express themselves in a way to indicate that they are persons of excellent sentiments and have a faculty for saying the right thing at the right time. Their philanthropic bent will always "make a fair show in the flesh." They like to meet and organize and adopt a constitution and by-laws with the right ring in them, and then elect a president and several vice-presidents. They hear addresses and discuss papers and eat

The Men who Look On

big dinners, and pass resolutions and make reports. And then, after five years of talk, and after going through all these motions, perchance they have done nothing or next to nothing at setting the world right. The wounded man is still there suffering, and they pass by on the other side to attend another public meeting in the interest of reform down at Jericho.

I believe heartily in agitation, consultation, education, but always with some practical end clearly and constantly in view. It must all look toward something, and be actually moving upon it. It must mean business. One of the perils is that some of the present day charities and reforms are in danger of becoming fads. They serve as an outlet for pent-up emotions; they create centers of social intercourse with something to give point; they relieve the monotony of many a sated and useless life. They form a parade ground where the sensibilities may don their blue coats and brass buttons, and, by marching and countermarching, ac-

Two Parables

quire a feeling that the hosts of want and wretchedness are being put to flight. But they often stop short of handling and relieving the wounded, bloody, dusty men at the roadside, whose interests they profess to have at heart. We cannot expect to touch bottom instantly in our relief work; and we must, of necessity, make our way through heaps and piles of routine up to the real business in hand. But if we form the habit of thinking that we must be making the world better, because we are studying its ills, and talking pathetically over the direful necessity that something should be done, and passing resolutions condemning the robbers who are off in the rocks and never read them, then we are Levites, one and all. We have simply looked on and left the real work we are sent to do, off to the side.

The idle exercise of pity anywhere quickly shades off into sheer self-indulgence. There are people who take great comfort in weeping with those that weep, simply for the

The Men who Look On

sake of the experience. They are very forward at funerals, and even when they do not know the family, will count it so much better to be in the house of mourning than in the house of feasting, that they will not fail to be conspicuously in evidence. Ministers and undertakers come to know them as professional funeral goers, who take morbid satisfaction in looking upon sorrow and passing by on the other side. In other walks of life, they hire a policeman and go "slumming." They find an unnatural pleasure in going down and seeing vice, squalor, wretchedness, which they have not come to reform or relieve, but merely to look upon; and then they calmly draw their skirts away and pass it by. They are the first cabin passengers who will ask permission to go down into the steerage, where the poor emigrants, in their first stages of loneliness and seasickness, in the meagerness and discomfort of their situation, are indeed objects of pity. They will openly exclaim over the lot of these "poor creatures," until they bring down the wrath of the captain on their heads and are shut out of all parts of the ship but their own. In every case it is the Levite disposition that likes to come close to misery, study it, collect the statistics, photograph it with a kodak, and, with no effort at or purpose of practical relief, pass it by. How ugly and how hateful it all is!

The same spirit has invaded literature. Zola and Hardy and Hall Caine have been giving us what they call realistic fiction. It often means that they go down and take the vicious elements of society in their crude animalism, and introduce them into the parlor and the study. To what end? It may serve some useful purpose in awakening us to the need of social betterment — God makes the mistakes and even the wrath of men to praise Him at times. "There is some soul of goodness in things evil, would men observingly distil it out;" but undistilled, the grosser details of vice and misery are not wholesome, edifying reading

The Men who Look On

for the miscellaneous public. Mission workers, students of penology, and those who seek statistics for scientific charity and reform, need to come close and know things as they are. But the great outside world, that has no ability nor wish to deal with the mysteries of Whitechapel or the vices of Paris, or the wretchedness of the other half in New York, has no more right to wade through this slough of fiction than it has to make personal visits to the pest-houses in fever-stricken Memphis. It is a bent and twisted element in our human nature that prompts us to look upon pain and sin with no other purpose than to simply see it, and then pass by on the other side.

Any unnecessary exercise of the emotional nature with no definite end in view, is a mere wasteful abuse of one's self. We are always suspicious of these people who talk to us of the great moral uplift they receive from the modern theater. It is easy to understand how bright, clean, sensible plays can have a rightful place in a Christian civilization, for purposes of recreation. Life is not all work, nor all worship; part of it must, of necessity, be pure play. But those plays framed with the idea of appealing to the moral nature, where the heavy villain goes on plotting successfully against the innocent maiden and her high-minded lover, but is at last exposed and brought to nought, so that virtue comes out triumphant as the curtain is rung down—they serve no good end. The moral fibre, built up by the exercise of pity, sympathy and gratification at such times, is weak and flabby. People whose emotions are not sufficiently exercised by coming in contact with the painful realities of life, feel the need of a little extra rubbing and emotional massage from this painted exhibition of human trouble. They often fancy that they must be making moral progress because they have wept a little, and felt a little hot indignation at the villain, and cheered enthusiastically when it all came out right in the end.

The Men who Look On

Then they calmly put their opera-glasses in the case and draw their furs around them, and pass out to live just as they were living before. Sturdy self-sacrifice, deep consecration to duty, and an unflinching loyalty to a high Christian ideal, must be fed upon something more robust than the gentle stirring of the emotional nature by these painted and acted troubles. The melodramatic and tragical performances that arouse people and lead them to look upon human grief and pain, and then send them by on the other side, serve simply to recruit the army of idle Levites.

Few things in this fallen nature of ours are more discouraging than the willingness to look idly and indifferently upon the distress and degradation of others. Why do thousands clamor to see a wretched murderer hung? Why does it pay the newspapers to print columns of the nauseating details? They are not in the printing business for their health, nor as a pastime; they print these accounts of hangings only be-

Two Parables

cause there is a hungry public ready to buy and read. A few years ago, a celebrated criminal in Philadelphia made a notable confession. He owned up to having committed some twenty-seven murders, and he recounted all the ghastly details. A fabulous sum was paid for this forty-two column confession by one of the "enterprising journals." It was printed in the Sunday issue, and served up to a wide constituency. After it was all over the murderer made another confession, stating that it was all a fake, as to nearly every one of the instances of crime, and was gotten up simply to make money for him and for the paper. What a spectacle! A great reading public standing by and paying its money simply to be guyed and fooled. It all arose from the nasty habit of finding gratification in coming over and looking upon crime, only to pass by on the other side.

On the streets of Boston I once saw a drunken woman arrested. She was about fifty years of age, a wife and a mother.

The Men who Look On

She became noisy and troublesome, and the policeman rang for the patrol-wagon. A great crowd collected. Boston is a busy city, but hundreds of people could pause in their activity to see a drunken woman taken to the jail. The curious and almost joyous interest in the face of the crowd was an ugly sight. When the woman was actually in the patrol-wagon, she was frantic, and struggled to throw herself out. It became necessary for the sturdy officer to seat himself beside her, and, placing his arm around her, to hold her in by force, while they were driving off. When the crowd saw that, a great shout of amusement and derision went up! The pathos of it, the utter degradation of one like in sex and form to our own mothers, the terrible tragedy in that woman's home and family—all this was lost on them! The scene in the patrol-wagon was ugly; the look on the face of the crowd was even worse. Our Master would have stooped down and looked upon the ground as though He saw her not. These modern representatives of what should be a Christian civilization, cheered and jeered and viciously rejoiced at the unwonted sight.

There is also a certain speculative charity, which looks upon and thinks upon, writes and talks about the needs of the world, and then passes along. Mrs. Booth, in speaking of certain books which were being widely read, "Darkest England," "The Bitter Cry of Outcast London," and "How the Other Half Lives," said that the criticism of the next century upon our time will be: "How perfectly the people of that day saw their problem; how imperfectly they solved it." A mere speculative interest in charity, indeed, works an additional condemnation upon us, just in proportion to the thoroughness of its recognition of the need. If the Levite had not seen the wounded traveler at all, he would not have been guilty of that neglect. So that for our own peace of mind, the only allowable excuse for looking upon human suffering, directly or through

The Men who Look On

our reading, must be to gain facts and motives for practical relief work.

One reason why we dread excessive organization, in church and outside of it, is that people quiet their consciences and satisfy that demand for some kindly activity, which God has implanted somewhere in most of us, by going through certain motions in the organization. If you are president of some relief society and secretary of some guild for vagrants, and if you helped to frame the constitution for the rag-carpet society, you feel that you must be helping on the good cause of charity, even though you may never have actually done any real Samaritan-like work. In my father's barn on the old farm there was a heavy cornsheller which, as a boy, I was not able to turn if there was any corn in it. But when the machine was empty and the coast was clear, I used to like to go in and turn the crank and make the empty cornsheller go around with a great noise. And, with a boy's active and joyous imagination, I could easily fancy

Two Parables

that the process of cornshelling was in actual operation. I would order imaginary men to bring in more corn, and other imaginary men to carry away the corn already shelled and to remove the cobs. The whole process was taking place for me, even though the machinery was running entirely empty. Some of the well meant relief work of our own day is almost as ineffective. The paraphernalia and the machinery and the roar are all there. The motions and the conversations are all gone through with, but oftentimes the plant is running empty; no real wants are being relieved. Social betterment is thus sometimes held back, not by open hostility, nor by flat indifference, but by an empty show of interest.

Another charge may be justly brought against the habit of looking idly upon the distress of others. Jesus had a grave purpose in telling us not to sound a trumpet before us when we do our alms. It was not simply a shaft aimed at the vulgar display of one's benevolence; it was also a pro-

The Men who Look On

tecting arm thrown around those whose necessities compel them to receive alms. For their sake, let there be no display. The poor have fine feelings and sensibilities, just as they have feet and hands. They are made very much as we are. With all rightly constituted people, it is a more blessed and a much more enjoyable experience to give than to receive. So that the charity worker, privately or officially, has need of the utmost tact, skill, and thoughtful consideration. It is possible to feed the stomachs of the poor, and at the same moment to torture their minds and hearts. If the caution of Jesus, then, against calling unnecessary attention to the wants of others when we are actually relieving them was demanded, how much more stern would be His rebuke of those who go to look upon distress only to pass by on the other side.

One winter, in the city of New York, we had an exhibition of spectacular charity sufficient to disgust all Christian sentiment. A few weeks after the Holidays it was pro-

Two Parables

posed to have a sort of belated Christmas-tree, for the neglected boys and girls in the Bowery district. The Fifth Avenue children were asked to give of their toys, those they had tired of, or those that had become slightly broken,—those that could be spared as well as not. A great hall was hired, the tree hung thick with the presents donated by these sated and jaded little benefactors, and the urchins of the Bowery were assembled for the distribution. Then, into the great galleries the rich children were brought to see with what eager pleasure these poor little fellows could receive what had been cast off by the well-to-do. The whole performance tending to bring out the prig and snob in those childish natures which, for a few years certainly, ought to be kept clean and innocent of such traits! All unnecessary and unseemly looking upon the straits of a fellow-being is bad for us and bad for him. It puts us into the company of the condemned Levite.

There is a speculative, onlooking interest

The Men who Look On

in politics, too, that enrolls its quota of Levites. These intense lovers of purer municipal government are willing to read the "Nation" regularly and applaud mightily when some pungent orator will score the ward bummers and the bosses. They can hold up their hands unto heaven in pious horror at the doings of Tammany and Dick Croker. They can beat upon their breasts, and rend their garments, and throw dust upon their heads at the very mention of the iniquities at the City Hall. But somehow they lack stomach and zeal to get down from their high horses of condemnation and do the bloody, dusty work of getting the robbed, wounded and helpless city government on its feet. They are not willing to grapple with primaries and caucuses, with ward organization or personal effort in the precinct. They come over and look upon the distressing situation, and then critically pass by on the other side.

There is also a speculative regard for Christianity which looks upon the subject of religion only to pass quickly on. Ian Maclaren, in his Yale Lectures, was speaking of the interest in theology. He avers that while some ministers claim that the average audience has little or no interest in theological questions, the publishers know better. In fiction, three of the most widely-read volumes were, "The Story of an African Farm," "John Ward, Preacher," and "Robert Elsmere," each dealing with a problem in theology. And three of the widely-read solid books have been Balfour's "Foundations of Belief," Drummond's "Ascent of Man," and Kidd's "Social Evolution"—all theological in their main bent and contention. Draper's "History of the Conflict Between Religion and Science" has passed through more editions than any other volume in the International Scientific Series. These facts he adduces to show that if a man will deal with theological questions in a thorough-going and understanding way, he has the wind with him.

But much of this is only a superficial,

The Men who Look On

speculative interest, and does not warrant great hopes for the enlargement of Zion as a consequence. People have a theoretical interest in many questions of faith. They would readily attend a heated debate on Heaven and Hell between two fierce opponents, but with no thought of gaining additional help for avoiding the one and reaching the other. If a minister rushes into print, and in an open letter to the newspaper attacks some brother minister's theology, and endeavors to shatter his reputation for orthodoxy; and if the attacked minister sends back a hot reply, and then our heresy-hunter comes in with a red-hot rejoinder, much interest of a certain sort may be stirred up in the community. Many will read and discuss the articles whose interest in religion is next to nothing, and which is in no wise increased by this little joust. What a gust of heated talk we had last winter over a remark President Jordan chanced to make about revivals! Many people read the attacks and replies, who

Two Parables

never thought of attending the revival then in progress, for the sake of deepening their own moral and spiritual lives. Their interest in the whole discussion was merely speculative; they came and looked on, and passed by on the other side.

One of the notions we have to combat is that religion can be confined to the opinions of the head and the feelings of the heart; that a man can carry on quite a religious life, and never come down to the plane of concrete and definite action. Some people imagine that repentance is feeling bad over their faults, crying a little perhaps, wishing they were better, instead of being what it is in the Word of God, facing about, making restitution to those we have wronged, and starting morally on a new tack. And faith is regarded as a feeling or opinion rather than as a steady reliance upon God, and a confident expectation that His grace and help will come to us increasingly as we seek to do His will in the practical affairs of life. These

The Men who Look On

people treat religion as a thing to be thought about and felt about, to be looked upon with the mind and with the heart, and then to be passed by when the hour has come for definite action.

Jesus describes a certain set of surprised and disappointed people who will appear at the last day. They will come, saying, Lord, Lord, have we not been intensely interested in the subject of religion; have we not prophesied in Thy name; and in Thy name cast out devils, and in Thy name done many wonderful works? Name, name, name! That same showy, specious, canting use of the name of God that we abhor to-day. They cannot open their mouths without using the name. And Jesus will answer them, Not every one that thinks about religion with his head or talks about it with his mouth; not every one that saith unto Me, Lord, Lord, in ever so many places and ever so many times, shall enter into the Kingdom of Heaven, but he that doeth the will of my Father who is in Heaven. Religion, to be religion at all, must come down to the plane of practical life.

There is a crowd of people in every community whose main interest is religious. They always want to hear the last word on religion. If a new minister comes to town, they must hear him at once. If some speaker has a new doctrine or fad to promulgate, they will go and receive his word with great joy for a while, sitting well up in front. If some man should announce that he would preach in evening dress, or standing on one foot, or that he would discuss some freaky topic, this coterie will be there. They will sit with minds and mouths wide open, and take both away as empty as they came. Their chief concern is to look upon all phases of religion, and then to pass by on the other side without any active or continued participation in the real work of Christ's kingdom. The valiant captain of this host is the Levite of the parable.

Sometimes I look at you, as I presume every minister looks at his congregation now

The Men who Look On

and then, and say to myself, Why talk to you any more on the subject of religion? You already know more than you are even attempting to practice. You understand more of the will of God than you really obey. And what is true of you is equally true of the minister. Why not stop talking, go and do what we know for a time, and when we have succeeded, we shall then be hungry to learn more about religion. If the whole purpose of this service was instruction, that might be valid advice. Our worship, however, brings moral stimulus and invigoration for doing the will of God. But let me beseech you not to be found in the number of those who stand and look reverently, thoughtfully, and even sympathetically on the subject of religion, and then pass by on the other side. May the truth and grace and spirit of God summon you all away from the side of the Levite, and enroll you with the Samaritan! May you learn the will of God, and then go and do, that you may live!

The Man on Horseback

"A certain Samaritan . . . . went to him and bound up his wounds . . . . and set him on his own beast."

You know the facts of the situation as well as you know your own names. Those Bedouins that hide among the hills between Jerusalem and Jericho, had set upon a traveler, taken all he had, stripped him, wounded him in the struggle, leaving him half dead. Presently a priest came along, and afterward a Levite. They saw the poor traveler lying there. It was too bad, but it would be a very disagreeable piece of work to get him up, bloody and helpless as he was, and take him to an inn. Besides, they were in a great hurry to get down to Jericho. And it was through no fault of theirs that the man got into trouble; it was very imprudent of him to travel alone on that dangerous road. So

The Man on Horseback

they excused themselves and passed by on the other side. Then a certain Samaritan rode up. Samaritans were not in good theological odor at that time; they even rejected all the Old Testament except the first five books. They were far from being orthodox and sound in the faith. But heretic as he was, the Samaritan felt sorry for that poor traveler. He got off and went to him. He bound up his wounds, pouring in a little of his olive oil and wine to make the bandages soft. He finally got the man up "and set him on his own beast" and took him along to an inn.

This picture Jesus hung up in the New Testament for our instruction. When the lawyer asked what he should do to inherit eternal life, Jesus showed him the picture and said, "Go and do thou likewise." It is a good picture to hang on the walls of your mind. It will tell you what Christian service is. It is personal; it is self-sacrificing. It gets off and walks to let a needier man ride. It walks beside him, steadies him, holds him on, and helps him to use what has been offered him. It is ready to suffer delay and inconvenience. It will take hold of men who are bloody and dusty, and become bloody and dusty itself in order to help them. It is never content to ride along comfortably and harmlessly; it must lift up some helpless man and bring him to a place of safety.

I called this sermon "The Man on Horseback" with no thought of getting a catchy or sensational title. It simply describes the man I want to preach to this morning. The most of us are mounted. We may not be riding in a coach and six, but we have at least a small Syrian donkey under us. We have money—some more, some less; all of us more than enough for actual needs. We have good homes—not palaces, perhaps, but places of peace and comfort—and it is a great help to a man in making the journey of life to be mounted on a good home. We have some intelligence, some knowledge of what life is and what can be made out of it—not so much real wisdom as we wish, but enough to be of great service to us. We have some measure of goodness—nothing prancing or showy, but, like the Samaritan's donkey, plain, quiet, useful everyday goodness, that aids us mightily in making our way from Jericho up to Jerusalem.

As we ride along on these advantages of ours, we see men by the roadside who somehow have been robbed, wounded, and are really helpless and half dead. Heredity robbed, stripped and wounded some of them. This unreliable man's father was a liar, and the boy was born with his tongue twisted. That unsteady fellow had a drunkard for a father, and he began life with an unnatural thirst. These other unfortunates are shiftless, but they were born, cradled and reared in a family atmosphere that had oxygen and nitrogen in it, but lacked energy, thrift and grit. There they are, scattered all along life's roadway! They will never be able to make the journey without some friendly lift. You cannot assist them all; perhaps you can do as the Samaritan did, and share your advantage with one. The moment you get down and set some helpless man upon your own beast, you begin to travel on the way to eternal life.

We have a soft proverb that people who are morally sleepy and lazy often lie down upon: "Live and let live." It teaches you that it is a man's business to live honestly, truthfully, respectably, and let others live the same way, if they can. It is a weak, low conception. It is no great thing for a man well mounted at the start, with a healthy body, a clear head and a reasonably pure heart, to go out and live a successful life. He may not become a millionaire or go to Congress, but if he is industrious, the results of his life will add up well. A healthy man could easily ride his donkey from Jerusalem to Jericho, robbing no one, wounding nobody by running over him— simply riding and letting ride. But that is

The Man on Horseback

not the way to inherit eternal life. The man who rides up to the gate of heaven comfortably mounted on his advantages, which he may indeed have bought and paid for, but which he has not used on the road in aiding helpless men to find their way to the gate of heaven, too, will find the gate shut. The very essence of Christianity is the willingness to get down off of some advantage, which rightfully belongs to us, and set some helpless man upon it. That is the doctrine of the parable. It is the doctrine Paul teaches. "Have this mind in you, which was also in Christ Jesus." Being in the form of God, he counted it not a prize to be on an equality with God, but emptied himself, taking the form of a servant, and, being found walking on the ground beside us, in fashion as a man, he gave himself for us in all his ministry of life and death.

We often get hazy ideas about consecrating ourselves to God. We fancy it is some dim, mysterious transaction that takes place

Two Parables

in our souls when we are in consecration meeting, or while we are bowed in prayer. We can form the purpose of consecration at that time, and ask God to witness and confirm our purpose; but the consecration itself must be done on the road. Consecration means "devoted to a sacred use." Our communion cups and plates are consecrated vessels, not because they are made of a different sort of silver from that in the spoons we eat with, or the dollars in our pockets, but because of the use to which we devote them. The moment the Samaritan got off and began to care for the wounded traveler, the bandages, the oil and wine, his own beast, his own strength, and skill, and thought and love, all became consecrated. Consecration is the act or the habit of taking our powers and devoting them to the service of God by using them for the service of men.

Jesus knew how easily men would forget what a social and neighborly thing religion is, and He strewed all through His teachings

The Man on Horseback

these reminders, that we inherit eternal life by using our powers to minister to human need. Such life is eternal life, because it knows the true God and Jesus Christ whom He has sent, through obedient fellowship. How ugly is the sight of a person who thinks that the chief end of man is to save his own soul, and enjoy the results of it forever! He picks out some well-made statement of belief with a strong back, that it may not break down under him, and saddles and bridles it with certain experiences through which he is confident he has passed, and then mounts it and rides along serenely toward what he believes to be the new Jerusalem. He may feel sorry for those poor fellows to the right, who are down, helpless, and half dead in their unbelief. He has pity for the others on the left, who have been robbed and wounded by their sins. He offers a prayer for them, or, perhaps, hands them a tract as he passes by; but he rides on, comfortable and secure in his own moral and spiritual advantages.

Two Parables

That man's religion is vain, and the name of the place he will reach is not Jerusalem.

If the Samaritan had simply jogged along down to Jericho, transacted his business, paid his bills, returned to his home to live faithfully and respectably with his wife, robbing and wounding none, but ignoring those who had been wounded and robbed, he would never have found place in the New Testament. His path would not have been pointed out as the way to inherit eternal life. Some men will ride up to the gates of another world, and when asked as to what they have done, the reply will be, We worked and bought a house and lot; we put in furniture and books and pictures; we had membership in the club, good standing in society, and a good pew in church. We mounted these advantages and rode them through, never injuring any one. Then the question will come, Where are the helpless men you saw by the way? Where are the sinful ones you might have won for Christ? Where are the struggling boys who might have been assisted in establishing themselves in business? Where are the confused souls to whom your clearer head might have brought light and faith? How many needy ones might have shared in your advantages and have been helped to make the journey, and yet you appear alone!

The Eastern legend said the gate of heaven was so narrow that one man walking alone could not pass through; two men walking side by side, one of whom had helped the other, found easy entrance; and when ten men came, who had all been serving one another in love, they found the gate so wide that they saw no post on either side.

The Samaritan's service was also intensely personal. We have gotten in so much religious and charitable machinery that we attempt to do a large part of our work at a distance. This story would have been very different if the Samaritan had seen the trouble and said, When I reach home I must send a check to the Relief Corps for wounded travelers; or if he had simply determined to get a ringing resolution passed at the next meeting of the association denouncing those "Bedouin atrocities;" or if he had consumed all his philanthropic zeal in writing "an open letter" to the paper on the "laxity of police regulations on the road from Jerusalem to Jericho." In the mean time, the poor, wounded, half-dead traveler would have been dead altogether. What the Samaritan did was to get off and take personal care of the needy man—after that, the check, the open letter, and the resolutions might be very well. But it was his doing something personal and definite that saved one man's life.

The best Christian service is handmade. In the Old Testament, when the woman's child was sick unto death, she sent for the prophet Elisha. He first sent his stick, with the command that it be laid on the child. But there was no recovery. He sent his servant Gehazi. At last he went himself, "and put his mouth upon his mouth, and his eyes upon his eyes, and his hands upon his hands, ... and the flesh of the child waxed warm." The sick and sinful human race will never be recovered until good men, after sending their sticks and checks, their servants and their committees, come themselves, and by close and personal service engage in saving that which is lost.

It is good for a man to have his name on the roll of the church; it shows the world where he stands in regard to the religion of our Lord Jesus Christ. It is good for him to send his check for the maintenance of public worship. It is good for him to be present at Sunday morning service. But we want the whole man, his voice, judgment, heart, personal friendship, sympathy; we want to enlist the total man in the service of Christ. We want him to grapple personally with the establishment of the Kingdom of God in Oakland, as the Samaritan grappled with the wounded traveler. We want the Christian man to take hold of the work of the church with his own hands, and think and plan with his own head, and love and pray with his own heart. We all believe that good is being accomplished by the regular ministry, by evangelists, and by many special agencies. But we believe that still more can be done by the plain people themselves. No single minister or evangelist, in this or any other pulpit, could do as much toward the establishment of the people of Oakland in Christian life as this body of unordained, untitled Christian men and women. The business man who has faced the world on its practical side for thirty years can show his young friend, in an unconventional talk, the value of Christian character. The woman who has traveled in her experience of womanhood all the way from May to December, and is not old yet, and never will be old, can show the young girl how nothing sweetens, strengthens and ennobles a woman's life like faith in God, the habit of

The Man on Horseback

prayer, and the unwavering purpose to make the atmosphere of her presence deeply Christian. We have trusted so much to set addresses and professional appeals! Jesus depended more upon personal, familiar, social intercourse and conversation for the growth of His kingdom. He talked with fishermen in their boats; He put forward the truth of God as He met people on the road, at the public wells, in the marketplace, and at their festivals and feasts. The work of Christianizing the world will be done best as we take hold personally, man by man, after the fashion of the Samaritan lifting the wounded traveler.

The professor of philosophy in an American university, a few years ago, felt that the churches in the town were not accomplishing for the students what needed to be done. In the public services there was no opportunity to talk back. Young people like to ask questions, make objections, demand reasons and proofs. He announced that he would be "at home" on Sunday afternoons. His parlors were large and would seat over a hundred students. His wife had studied abroad and was an accomplished musician. The young men and young women filled the parlors, glad to feel themselves in a home, delighted with the music, and, more than all, eager to discuss in frank, unconventional fashion such questions as confronted them: Why should we believe in the inspiration of the Bible? What is atonement, and how does it affect us? How does one begin a Christian life? What about studying on Sunday? What is the rational Christian course in regard to popular amusements? The discussions were without restraint or reserve, and the interest increased year after year. This professor saw that both the faith and the practice of many of the students was wounded and sometimes left half dead, by their absence from home, by their entrance into a new world, by their studies in science, in philosophy—by the larger outlook that clashed with some of the beliefs of childhood,

The Man on Horseback

which they had not taken pains to revise. Instead of riding comfortably along upon his house, and his intellectual attainments, and his own clear, rational, Christian belief, he dismounted on Sunday afternoon and placed them all at the disposal of these young friends. In this thoughtful and personal service, he showed that he had learned the way to inherit eternal life.

This passage also teaches us the worth and power of that plain kindness which has no fringe or border of religious exhortation. Some would say that Jesus left the parable incomplete. It seems almost perilous to point a man who is inquiring the way of eternal life to the simple kindness of the Samaritan, and then, without a single note of warning or apology touching his heresies, say, "Go, and do thou likewise." If the Samaritan, after getting the traveler to the inn, had talked to him about his soul, or had left him a copy of Walker's "Plan of Salvation," it might have been better. It seems risky to leave the account of his service so incomplete. But there it is; that is the way Jesus left it. Indeed, Christ sometimes showed a strange disregard for things we count of great moment. He began His public ministry at a wedding, and when the refreshments gave out He helped them to get some more. We are not told that He followed this kind act by any homily, or that he used it to point a moral. He graciously added to the joy of that occasion in Cana of Galilee, and left it there; "and his disciples believed on Him." They had believed on Him before, but it deepened their faith as they saw Him come to the marriage that it might have joy and might have it more abundantly.

The power of plain kindness in social life is under-estimated. We are slow of heart to believe that real religious business can be transacted while we are in our swallow-tail coats and our light gowns. We will suppose that you are mounted upon a wide acquaintance in society; that you have acquired the poise, balance, and presence of

The Man on Horseback

mind that is invaluable in social life; you know enough not to bore people with long stories; you manage your conversation as a sailor sails his boat, holding the rope in one hand, the rudder in the other, watching and utilizing every puff of wind. You have the quick sense and the light touch of a member of society in good and regular standing. It is easy for you to ride along on these advantages and have a good time at any party or reception. You will make the journey from one end of the evening to the other without a jar or a dull moment. But on the roadside, hard against the wall perhaps, are others who are shy and awkward; or they are loud or tiresome, and in consequence they are politely but firmly avoided. You may ride by on the other side; or you may get down off of your happiness and walk more slowly in order to bring others who feel helpless along with you to the place where society shall have for them as well, its full meaning and pleasure. Simple, watchful, thoughtful kindness is always in good form; there are times and places where it will accomplish more than sowing the pathway thick with tracts and exhortation. It is a language we can all understand; it translates the message of peace and good will into a tongue wherein all men were born; and when you are living to minister rather than to be ministered unto, you are putting the essence of Christian life before men in its most persuasive form.

A man in my study this week referred to one of our church members, and said, "Mr. Blank is a beautiful Christian." Then he went on to speak of the beauty of his Christian life. It was not that he had heard him pray so well in prayer-meeting, or give some ungodly fellow such a good talking to, or utter such a stout defense of some cardinal doctrine. He had camped out with him. He told me that Blank was always doing something for somebody else. He was helping them to organize their picnic and get off. He was helping to get the lunch put up. He was aiding this man in getting his fishing tackle in shape. He was doing a Benjamin's portion of the plain, ordinary camp work. When his friends remonstrated with him, and insisted that he should go and enjoy himself, his invariable reply was, "I am enjoying myself; I like this." He had learned to get off and help others, and so to walk joyously in the way of eternal life. He had meat to eat that some men know not of, because his meat was to do the will of Him that sent him.

Finally, the Samaritan consecrated what he had. He "set him on his own beast." An ambulance would have been better, or even a carriage, or two men with a stretcher, but he had none of these; he had one small Syrian donkey, and such as he had, he gave to the service of the wounded man. The streets are swarming with people to-day who would endow colleges and build churches and establish hospitals, if they were millionaires. This church is full of people now who would teach in Sunday-school and speak in prayer-meeting and engage actively in Christian work, if they had "a talent for it." How ready they are to give what they cannot give; how tardy they are about giving in glad consecration such as they have.

"Silver and gold have I none," said Peter. It was silver and gold the lame man asked, and his face fell. "But such as I have, give I thee," added the apostle; and that gave the situation a new look. We always attach importance to what a man has, rather than to what he has not. The question is not what you would do with a drove of Arabian horses or a procession of carriages, if you had them; but what you are ready to do now, right here on the road, with the one Syrian donkey that you have. You can begin to use it at once in serving the needs of men. You are riding this morning on some advantages, some knowledge, some abilities, that can be used to bless and help the world, and your possession of eternal life depends

The Man on Horseback

upon what you mean to do with "such as you have."

I have spoken strongly regarding the power of self-sacrificing kindness. My Master spoke strongly. The most sanguine words Jesus ever uttered touching the prospects of His Kingdom were these: "And I, if I be lifted up from the earth, will draw all men unto Me. This He said, signifying what death He should die." It was the sober estimate of the Son of God as to the power of self-sacrificing love.

Unto the End

"Take care of him; and whatsoever thou spendest more, when I come again I will repay thee."

Some of you are here this first Sunday of the New Year, all fresh and sweet in your new suits of good resolutions. And even those of you who brand the habit of swearing off in certain directions and swearing on in others as foolish, somehow have a feeling as if you had taken a fresh start in life. As far as eighteen hundred and ninety-eight goes, you have not committed a great deal of sin; you have attended church every Sunday; you have really pitched your thought and aspiration in a higher key. You have a general purpose, clear here, vague there, to make this the best year you have ever lived. So right now, while you are in this rosy, expectant mood, I want to preach to you

Unto the End

about the everlasting importance of bringing our undertakings to something like successful completion. Not he that maketh forty gallant and enthusiastic beginnings, but "he that endureth to the end shall be saved!" It is an encouraging fact that you can look at your purposes and determinations this morning and say, "Thus far I have run well." It will be necessary, however, for you to wait until you can add, "I have fought a good fight; I have finished my course; I have kept the faith," before you will be confident that there is laid up for you a crown of righteousness. So my theme this morning will be, "Unto the End."

To get this lesson well down into our minds and hearts, perhaps we cannot do better than to spend another half hour with our old friend, the Samaritan. He, too, was a man of fine purposes, kindly instincts, excellent sentiments, and full of general good will toward men. As he rode along that morning on the Jericho road, it would have done you good to look at him —and if you could have looked into him, that would have been still better. But he was more than a beautiful embodiment of splendid purposes. When he came around the bend in the road and saw that wounded traveler, his good will leaped off and ran to the sufferer; his noble purposes began to tear up bandages and pour in oil and wine. His kindly instincts began to lift that dusty, bloody stranger up and get him on his own beast, that he might take him to an inn. Next morning, the traveler having been robbed of his money, the Samaritan paid the bill for both. Then he gave orders that the good work should not stop there. The wounded man would not be able to travel for some time, but the Samaritan would see him through. "Take care of him, and whatsoever thou spendest more, I will repay thee." He carried his good work through unto the end.

In this day, when we see so much good-natured, promiscuous smattering, it is stimulating to look at such a picture of thoroughness. Sometimes men are so busy now that they have no time to do anything —that is, to actually do it. We have bungling artisans who have never learned their trades; never will learn them, they are so busy bungling. We have half-done men in all the professions; doctors killing their patients, lawyers making unnecessary fees for their clients, ministers making the Gospel seem ridiculous by their way of presenting it. We have would-be artists mixing and daubing, who have never learned to draw a clean, straight line that you can look at with comfort. We have people who fancy they are great readers, because they scamper through half a dozen newspapers a day, and skim over a long list of magazines, and glance through an armful of books every month. They are so out of breath that they cannot tell you much about what they have read, and they have not sufficient mental vitality to give birth to a single thought of their own that could stand alone. In religious study, some people are almost smothered by the quantity of lesson helps, side lights, illustrative applications, so that a man may not get a look at his own religious convictions in their bare, warm reality, once a month. In religious activity, we have so many irons in the fire, that there is peril lest it become all irons and no fire. In the midst of all this superficial haste, it is imperative that we stop now and then to realize the necessity of bringing something to measurable completeness. The efforts of our life which will be fruitful and creditable, will be those that we have, in a real sense, brought to a finish.

We are aware of the elementary and preparatory character of all forms of life in this world. Our work and our religious belief and our inner lives at best, must be regarded as unfinished in the light of their future possibilities. These mortal attainments must put on their immortality by emerging at last into a greater fullness.

Unto the End

But there is a sense in which we are to aim at, and to attain something like completeness. We are to strive, as Jesus said, to bring our work and our belief and our inner life to the point where they will be perfect, complete, round, even as the life of our Father which is in heaven is round. In that sense I speak to you about carrying your undertakings unto the end, whatsoever thou spendest.

Suppose there had been a wounded traveler every quarter of a mile along that Jericho road. The Samaritan might have paid a hurried visit to each one. He could have torn his bandages small, giving each a piece as large as my hand; he could have spared half a teaspoonful of oil and wine for every man. He could have uttered a few scraps of commiseration to each unfortunate before he hurried ahead to the next one. In that way, he might have added to the momentary comfort of them all and have reported that night in some Jericho meeting, that during the day

Two Parables

he had visited and comforted eighty-seven wounded travelers. In the mean time, they would all have died from chill and exposure and loss of blood. As it was, he selected one man, who had been robbed, wounded and left half dead, and, however many other sufferers there were in the world, he took care of *him* and saved his life.

Now, the Jericho road that we travel in our busy city life is just lined with cases that appeal to us for help. Every ten rods there is a man out of work, or a widow and her children in want, or an aged person with no friend to help. The appeals for assistance are with us in our down sitting and in our uprising. Every time you sit down there are two circulars for you to read, calling your attention to some cause, and asking your subscription. Every time you get up, four people meet you, to ask your help along some other lines. There are three courses open. One is to decide that there are so many, you cannot give to them all, you cannot even look into them

Unto the End

all to ascertain if they are deserving; you will give to none of them, and so shut the door in all their faces. A few cold-blooded, selfish people may do that. Or, you may decide that while you cannot look into them all, you will give a little to each one, remembering how we are told that it is better to encourage nine frauds than to pass by on the other side of one case of real desert. You give only a little; five cents to the beggar at the corner, five cents to the fellow at the back door, a dollar here and a dollar there, as the appeals come, reflecting that you are casting your bread upon the water and upon all the water in sight, and that surely some of it will drift around to the right place. Many kind-hearted, thoughtless, incompetent people do that. Then there is the third and right way, which is to select out of the crowd of appeals, certain objects of charity, certain needy persons, and look into them and know about them. And then, when you have ascertained the justice and the propriety of their claims, whatever you spend of time, of money, and of love, take care of them.

Much of our kindness becomes almost useless because it stops short of any valuable result. It is alleviative, but it does not look toward reconstruction. It would be right in the face of an unusual emergency; it is not right in the face of an ever-pressing problem which calls for some more permanent solution. If ten families give food to ten hungry men at the back door to-night, and let them go, the ten men will all be hungry again to-morrow morning. Ten more kind and credulous families on some other street will have to give them lunch, and ten more similarly-disposed families will have to be found by the dinner hour. After three weeks of this promiscuous benevolence, we are no farther along, no nearer a solution of the problem the ten men bring us, than we were at the start. If, on the contrary, one family would take one man, and turning a deaf ear to the other nine, seek to find work for him, and stay by him until he is restored to self-support, we should advance. And in the event of his being found unwilling to work, they should decline to do anything and allow him to sit out and grow thin, until, through such fasting and meditation, he might be born into a new sense of his relation to the industrial world. If one family would take any one case of need, and acquainting itself with the facts, and prosecuting its endeavors to a real result, take care of it, we should make progress. If a city likewise goes on doling out relief year after year, taking no steps to put the poor in a position where, by wood yards, or laundries, or potato patches, they might earn their bread, it will not advance one inch toward the solution of the problem of poverty. At first, we should need to spend more time, more money and more intelligence, than as though we simply passed out the cold victuals; but whatever we spend, we shall be taking care of people and bringing our work to some desirable end.

The best work is always done where you select, and then say, whatever I spend, I will take care of something definite. There is a great mass of trouble and suffering in the world that you cannot relieve; but this man you have in hand, you can take care of him. You can see him through, and then be ready, by and by, for another man. You employers have young men in your employ—boys who are away from home; some of them more inclined to find the saloons than to find the churches; more apt to find the bad people interesting than the good people. You cannot rush out and shut up all the saloons, and destroy all wicked influences. Perhaps you have one young man whom, by your friendship, your kindly counsel, your Christian interest, you can keep in the right way. Or you look around and see the army of incompetents, and you decide to serve your day and generation by choosing a likely boy who has not the opportunity for an education. You send him through grammar school, high school, and then give him some training to fit him for a useful and honorable place in the world. Whatever you spend, you take care of him. Or you find some family struggling along, food enough, clothes enough, perhaps, but no books, no pictures, no wholesome papers in the home, no sense of family companionship. You resolve to consecrate your friendship with that family to the work of leading them into a brighter, better home life. It must come to that some time, somewhere. We shall not regenerate people by gathering them into halls and lecturing them, nor by bringing them into churches and preaching to them, unless we also reach them where they live and change the home environment. You feel powerless to renovate all Oakland, but you choose one family, and whatever you spend, you are determined to take care of it. By such determined and detailed effort as this, the kingdom comes which is to usher in a new heaven and a new earth.

The same method is demanded in the more spiritual work of bringing men to Christ. We find people who profess great interest in the conversion of the world. A stranger spoke recently in our Endeavor meeting as to how, in his zeal, he had visited sixty families the day before, asking them to come to Christ. You could see him popping in at one door, uttering some hasty, formal words of exhortation, and then popping out again to hurry on to the next. He called it preaching the Gospel to every creature, as if the universal commission had been laid on his individual shoulders. And we have devoted and zealous distributors of tracts, who know nothing of the many into whose hands they slip their little leaflets, and know little of what the tract contains save that it is filled with pious words. And this they term, "sowing the seed," quoting with comforting assurance the passage in Isaiah about the word not returning void. But such hasty and thoughtless work is not sowing the seed at all. Sowing the seed is putting seed into the ground under the surface where it will grow. Sowing spiritual seed is making a spiritual impression; it is touching the human heart below the surface with the truth which God has given us. It cannot be lightly or unadvisedly done. The sower who goes forth to sow has entered upon the noblest and the hardest work in the world. Really, the men and the women who do the most to Christianize the world are the ones who strive to see to it that first of all their own children become useful, intelligent, devoted Christians. Then they enlarge the circle and include a small class of boys or girls in the Bible School, perhaps, or a few personal friends. In every case, the purpose is not to utter a few chance words to a hundred careless hearers, but to write a deep and lasting record of spiritual influence upon the few lives that offer us the sacred opportunity. You can

Two Parables

study and pray and acquire such a rational and comprehensive knowledge of scriptural religion that you will be enabled to take a few growing minds and equip them with a set of religious ideas that will become an abiding part of their religious natures. You can build within them something that will endure unto the end. The words our Saviour pronounced upon effective service, you remember, were not "well begun," nor "beautifully half done," but, "Well done, good and faithful servant, enter into the joy of thy Lord."

When General Grant was ordered East and put in command of the Union armies during the Civil War, some of the Confederate officers were joking about it in the tent of General Lee. It amused them to learn that "the tanner from out west," as they called him, had been placed in command. They laughingly referred to the fact that he was not polished, nor scientific in the art of war. In the midst of the talk, General Lee, who had been at West Point

Unto the End

with Grant, looked up gravely and said, "I know this man. We must prepare for the worst. Grant will fight, and he will fight all the time, and he will keep on fighting, until one of us is hopelessly defeated." What a perfect prophecy it was! Grant started in to fight his way from the Rapidan to the James. The Wilderness, Spottsylvania, North Anna, Cold Harbor—battle after battle! He kept stubbornly at it. In words that sound strangely like those of Lee, he proposed to fight it out, and to fight it out on that line. He seemed to feel that the cause of the Union had been committed to him, and whatever he spent, he would take care of it. And he did.

This method of singleness and thoroughness received no finer illustration anywhere than in the life of our Lord. As He entered upon His public ministry, there were many things that needed to be done; there were many things that He could do. He might have commanded that stones be made bread, or He could have leaped from the pinnacle of the temple, and thus have won public attention and a certain sort of public confidence. He might have obtained the kingdoms of the world upon certain conditions. He could have put Himself in the field against the Roman Government at the head of a band of Hebrew patriots, who would have fought to the death for their country's freedom. He declined all these. He came to do a certain work, and He held Himself firmly, evenly, constantly to that. He steadfastly set His face to go to Jerusalem, to go to Calvary, to go anywhere that He must go, in order to accomplish His mission. He so completely fulfilled the purpose of His coming, that in His last prayer He could look up and say, "Father, the hour is come. I have glorified Thee on the earth. I have finished the work which Thou gavest Me to do." As He hung upon the cross, He could confidently declare, "It is finished!" However great the cost, He did what He came to

Unto the End

do, and brought His work to its own glorious completeness.

It is well said in the Scriptures, "to every man *his* work," and not twenty other men's. The ears are for hearing, and we never censure them for being utterly indifferent to the work of seeing; that is handed over to the eyes. When each member does its work and does it well, the body rejoices in its own well-rounded life. Men who are out of work often come to city pastors. One of the first questions we ask is, "What can you do?" "Oh, I can do anything," is the common reply. Then we know they can do nothing. No trade, no profession, no business well learned, no specialty, but a vague willingness to render uncertain and crippled service at anything that will give them bread! They inevitably become the industrial driftwood of all our cities. " 'Tis in ourselves that we are thus or thus." A young man came from the country to one of the cities in the middle west, to make his fortune, and went to a wise old merchant to ask his advice. The old man's first inquiry was, "What can you do and do well?" The young man rather smilingly replied, "I can make good pickles; I used to make them on the farm and for the country store. But of course I would not want to do that. I think I should like to be a lawyer, or a banker, or perhaps a writer on one of the city newspapers." The shrewd old merchant eyed him still more closely and replied, "If you can do one thing and do it well, bend all your strength to that—make pickles." The young man had the good sense to follow the counsel; his bottles are in the best larders all over the land to-day, and he has retired from active business with a solid fortune.

The dabblers and triflers contribute little to the real prosperity of the community, and they secure no permanent success for themselves. Concentration is a fundamental condition of genuine progress. The man who succeeds is the man who resolves to know as much about some one thing as can be known. The man who determines to learn to do some one thing so that it cannot be done better, will have a chance to do it, and at a profit. And in our Christian work as well, God loves and regards and rewards the spirit of thoroughness. Take hold somewhere and begin to turn out finished work. You can take three minutes in the prayer-meeting and resolve, by thought, and prayer, and study beforehand, that you will fill it full of something that will help and bless every soul present. You can take the spot where you sit now, and fill a little circle there full of genuine Christian fellowship, as it never has been filled before. You can know the people who worship near you. You can indicate, in all polite and gracious ways, to the strangers that we are glad to see them in our Father's house. You can turn your attention to some one of the many forms of practical work in which we are engaged as a church, and strengthen it by your gifts, your presence, your prayers, and your labors. Enter where you see an opening, and then stay until you have carried through some piece of honest Christian work unto the end.

I would plead for the same thoroughness in arriving at one's religious convictions. We have slowly passed out of the period where people regarded all important religious questions as being fully understood and settled. The whole doctrinal side of Christianity is being rethought and restated in the interests of life rather than in the interest of some preconceived system. The whole method of biblical interpretation is being revised to fit the facts of history rather than to fit some prearranged theory of inspiration; and to minister to religious experience rather than to fill the demand for some objective infallible standard. We are coming to believe that those interpretations of the teaching of Jesus and of the words of inspired men, which most inspire us, and which, by the test of time and of extended experience, prove to be

Unto the End

most fruitful in holy life and service, are the ones that will turn out to be correct. So that there is much readjustment and alteration going on in the relation of part to part in the great religious structure where we live.

One result of this enlargement has been a certain mental laziness on the part of some believers, who excuse their lounging position by claiming that since we cannot know the exact and absolute truth, a strenuous effort is hardly worth while. It is a superficial and cowardly claim. "We know in part," as Paul reminded us; but there is a part which we can know and live by, which we can bravely use for the glory of God and for the good of our brother men. There are points where we cannot come to final conclusions, and many of our convictions are subject to revision as further light falls upon the word and the work of God, from that light which lighteth every man that cometh into the world. All this is true; but it is no less true that it is possible for a serious man, striving to do the will that he may know the doctrine, and keeping his heart pure that he may see God, to come to a foundation that standeth sure. And on that foundation he can build something of infinite worth, of gold or of silver or of precious stones, that will abide the day of the coming of the Lord. Never be willing to give it up! Use time, and thought, and study, and prayer; but whatsoever you spend, take care that you know the truth that makes men free! No man can understand chemistry without looking into it; no man can work in electricity without a vast amount of study. No more can a religious man estimate the place and potency of divine grace, the method and ability of that power of God which is unto salvation, until he patiently and thoroughly seeks to know what may be known, by the revelation God has given us of Himself. Resolve to know Him in whom you are asked to believe, and to understand why you are warranted in committing your

Unto the End

eternal interests unto Him against that day. Whatever you spend in reaching your conclusions, it will repay you if you carry your effort to know the truth even unto the end.

What is true of work and of belief is equally true of that inner life which constitutes the real character of the man. As you read your Bible, you see how it welcomes and encourages the first stirrings of moral effort. It is as gentle as a nurse with the earliest beginnings of Christian life. But it also invites, nay, summons us to constantly aim at completeness of Christian character. It bids us increase in moral stature, and in spiritual wisdom, and in favor with God and man, until we come to a perfect man, to the measure of the stature of the fullness of Christ. It labors to establish men's hearts in unblamable holiness before God. It calls upon men to be strong in the grace that is in Christ Jesus, that men of God may be thoroughly furnished unto every good work. It seems to join hands with us, saying, "Let us go on; let us go on to perfection." These are but a few of the many high summons uttered in the word of God, for us to persevere, whatsoever we spend, even unto the end of holy life.

On this, the first Sunday of another year, may we not then dedicate ourselves anew to this high undertaking. There is that in most of you that claims kinship with the divine. It brought you here this morning, saying to every questioner, "Wist ye not that I must be in my Father's house." It looked up a moment ago claiming the attention of the Infinite, when it prayed and said, "Our Father." It will go out presently with a sense of mission from on high, discharging its duties and meeting its obligations, reinforced by the consciousness that it can say, "I must be about my Father's business." To that life within you which thus asserts its noble kinship, I would give this new year counsel. "Go on unto perfection!" Be ye at last complete as your Father which is in heaven is complete. Not the

Unto the End

purposes and aspirations of the first of January alone, but rather the finished results of the last of December, shall secure for you the place from which you are to go no more out. The day will declare it, the long day which leads up to the night that lies between us and an eternal morning. Whatsoever thou spendest, take care of that inner life, that when it cometh unto the end, it may be "accounted worthy to stand before the Son of Man," and to take its place among those "men which are made after the likeness of God."

PART II

"A certain man had two sons; and the younger of them said to his father, Father, give me the portion of goods that falleth to me. And he divided unto them his living. And not many days after, the younger son gathered all together and took his journey into a far country and there wasted his substance with riotous living. And when he had spent all there arose a mighty famine in that land; and he began to be in want. And he went and joined himself to a citizen of that country, and he sent him into his fields to feed swine. And he would fain have filled his belly with the husks that the swine did eat, and no man gave unto him. And when he came to himself, he said, How many hired servants of my father's have bread enough and to spare; and I perish with hunger. I will arise and go to my father, and will say unto him, Father, I have sinned against heaven and before thee, and am no more worthy to be called thy son; make me as one of thy hired servants. And he arose and came to his father. But when he was yet a great way off his father saw him and had compassion and ran and fell on his neck and kissed him. And the son said, Father, I have sinned against heaven and in thy sight and am no more worthy to be called thy son. But the father said to his servants, Bring forth the best robe and put it on him; and put a ring on his hand and shoes on his feet; and bring hither the fatted calf and kill it; and let us eat and be merry; for this my son was dead and is alive again; he was lost and is found. And they began to be merry."

The Sinful Demand for Separateness

"Father, give me the portion of goods that falleth to me."

The moment the younger son said that he became a prodigal. His heart was already in a far country, wasting the true substance of its life in wrongdoing; it only remained to take his body there to fulfill the expressed wish. He was already sending himself into the fields to feed life on its lower levels, and his better nature already "began to be in want." When any man separates himself from the normal relationships so that he may live detached; when he takes his portion of time and strength out from under the eye of the Father and away from the side of his brother man, he begins to put his life in that condition which this parable calls "lost" and "dead." No man *liveth* unto himself—

the very attempt to do it brings the death-sentence.

One of the first statements in the Bible about the well-being of man is that "it is not good that the man should be alone." It refers to something more than a man's need of a wife. It indicates that true life is, of necessity, social. No man can be a complete man by himself. He fulfills himself through his relations with others. The joy, strength and usefulness of your life consist in the fact that you are a son, a husband, a father, a neighbor, an employer, a citizen, a church member, a child of God. These are your relationships; they tell us that you are not alone. You could not be any one of these things by yourself. We satisfy our wants and we find the fields of our activity through the mediation of society. "So far as the individual is concerned, his highest good consists in making his life a part of other lives. For, both manward and Godward, a man is essentially a social being and his life is imperfect in the

The Sinful Demand for Separateness

same proportion as it is not in union with the life of others." Give me my portion, therefore, is a demand for the impossible, and it must end in disaster. So the impulse for separation, which claims its portion, only to take it off into a far country, is an impulse toward self-destruction. Presently the Father, in giving an account of the matter, must say sorrowfully, "This, my son, is lost and dead."

The illustrations of this truth are as extensive as the field of life. The leaf that plucks itself from the tree, ceasing to feed and to be fed by the tree, and to share in its total life, ceases to be a leaf. Dust it was and unto dust it returns when it parts with its real life by the demand for separateness. If the rosebud, just approaching its supreme beauty, should say, "Give me the portion of rosebush that falleth to me," and should cut off its special twig, the unfolding would stop. No branch can have life, to say nothing of having it in sufficient abundance to bring forth fruit, except it abide in the vine. And in the kingdom of the spirit, unless a man accepts and maintains the relation of loving obedience to God, and of useful service to his fellows, his life will not come to its power and fruitfulness. Only as he fulfills his part and is a useful function or member of that by which he lives, is he able to serve men and to glorify God; only as he does that, is he able to live a man's life.

All forms of what we call vice are but the outer manifestations of the selfish and the mean spirit. They flourish in the soil of the human heart that is base enough to say, Give me my coveted gratification, regardless of its effect upon the lives of others. The intemperate man will imperil his health of body and soul, the peace and prosperity of his home, his standing in society, and his fitness to work out an honorable success, all for the sake of tickling for a moment his own palate and of feeling an exhilarating warmth in his personal stomach. He has truly shrunk to small

The Sinful Demand for Separateness

proportions when he can say, Give me this, even though the other and larger interests are sacrificed. The claim has been made that the very beginning of all moral evil is the willingness to draw a tight circle around the small share of gratification that can fall to the personal account, thus ignoring the wider values that are involved. Certain it is that the man saying, Give me my portion, speedily becomes a low outcast, while the man saying, Make me a servant of the general good, becomes a beloved and honored son.

A man's habitual attitude toward the world in this regard, then, is of vital importance. Does he make his standing request, "Give me for my private and exclusive use, the portion of goods that falls to me as a result of my ability and industry?" If the keynote of his activity is "Give me," you have told us the character of the man. He may, indeed, never claim a penny that does not legally belong to him. He may use part of his portion in providing for his family.

Two Parables

He may give some of it to benevolent objects. But if he enters the business world simply saying, "Give me," he will certainly disregard others, and will crowd them to the wall if they are in his way. He will hire men, thinking more of what their service will do for him than of what his employ will do for them. He will move about spending his money so that it will gratify him without pausing to ask whether the activities set in motion are for the good of the community. His dominant note throughout will be like the demand of the prodigal, "Give me."

How different all that is from the utterance of our Lord! His command was when ye pray—and when ye live, for a man's prayer is not a prayer unless he tries to live as he prays—say, "Give us this day our daily bread." A Christian man will go into the world of industry asking for success and prosperity; asking it for himself and asking it, in the same breath, for his neighbor. As he buys and sells, as he employs and

The Sinful Demand for Separateness

discharges, he will be constantly saying, Give us. He looks not only upon his own things, but also upon the things of others. In the whole conduct of his life, as well as when he engages in the work of charity, he is taking his neighbor into account and actually loving him! The request he makes of the world about him is, not "Give him" nor "Give me," but "Give us." Jesus was too wise to ever tell men to love their neighbors and not themselves. That would be a false and impossible rule of conduct. Love your neighbors with yourselves. In the selection of principles and methods, make the whole attitude of your life and the social request you utter, not, Give me, but rather, Give us.

There are times when we all behave with one accord as Christians. The selfish demand, Give me, is easily subordinate to the nobler request, Give us. We do that in church. We do it at the table. In a well-behaved family each member very naturally feels that his own need must be supplied.

But there is also a constant watchful interest in having the needs of others supplied. The self-interest and the altruism are combined and balanced. Each is conscious that in the father's house there is bread enough and to spare for all the children, and even for the higher servants. For any one to seize upon and separate his portion in utter disregard of the others would put our eating on the same level with the feeding of animals. And when we have eyes to see and ears to hear, we shall recognize the fact that this big world is our Father's house. There is bread enough, and joy enough, and grace enough and to spare. All greedy, cruel selfishness is unseemly and unnecessary, and it is most hateful in the eyes of the Father. Each man will become a true man just in proportion as he organizes himself with other men and makes the real demand of his life, Give us—all the men and women with whom I am related—the daily bread that will satisfy our utmost needs.

The Sinful Demand for Separateness

The word "social" is, perhaps, being overworked. We have social Christianity, social aspects of religion, social service, social regeneration. It is overworked because there has been a long accumulation of tasks left undone. We have passed through the age of despotism when the monarch stood alone and said, Give ME. We are now passing through the age of individualism when in freedom and equality each man may say the same. We are entering upon the age of mutualism when the combined request of all will be, Give us. No man should desire a personal success, a personal happiness, a personal culture, or even a personal salvation, that does not also include and make contribution to the success, happiness, culture, and salvation of us all. The man who makes it his chief business to ask and carry off the portion that falls to him must give place to the man whose chief joy consists in the wide and gracious answers coming all the time to that nobler request for the social and corporate weal.

Two Parables

The procession where it is "every man for himself," is a procession managed and driven by the devil, who is at the rear for the express purpose of taking in the hindmost. Each for all and all for each, would be the Christian form of it. By this I mean no foolish or impracticable communism, but rather, under whatever form of industrial organism we may be living, the steady cultivation of a large-minded way of considering the effect of one's life upon the lives of others who are involved with us. A man may choose his business, treat his employer or his employé, select his amusements, spend his money, saying, Give me the objects of my desire, regardless of the effect of my activity; or, he may order all these parts of his life with reference to the welfare of those who become concerned with him in the effect of the transactions. One of the ugliest things in the rum business is the brute selfishness of it. The man on one side of the bar says, Give me the exultation that comes from semi-intoxica-

The Sinful Demand for Separateness

tion, regardless of the loss and disaster that come to my home. The man on the other side cries, Give me gain, even though he sees that it is the devil's own business, wrecking the health, reason, prosperity, family peace, and moral natures of those on whom he depends for custom. Nothing but the narrowest, coldest, lowest selfishness could seek its gain by such wanton disregard of the effects of one's business and life work.

One of the great objects of the work of Jesus was to teach us to take others into account. He wrote the word "my" in small letters, the word "our" in large capitals. To make His personal example a striking lesson, He held no property in His own right. Every pair of foxes in Palestine had a hole, and each pair of birds a nest; but the Son of Man had not where to lay His head. He did not command His first followers to copy this course to the letter. Following Christ is not wearing such clothing as He wore, or speaking the

Two Parables

language He spoke, or painfully imitating the outward details of His life. It is rather the gaining of His spirit, and the making of our lives into an expression of that spirit, with such clothing, and language, and industrial system as may be in vogue in our own day. But His aim in His ministry was to accustom us to say, "Our Father;" to work, saying, "Give us our daily bread;" to be patient with the faults of others, saying, "Forgive us our faults;" and to hold such an attitude toward the things that make for evil as would say plainly, "Lead us not into temptation, but deliver us." The whole aim was to give us a sense of our corporate life and to set us praying, thinking, and working for the good of all. This social aspect of religion is said to be peculiar to Christianity. We are often told that one man and God could give us an illustration of many religions, because there a man's religion consists entirely in his relation to the object of his worship. His prayers, his observances, and his ceremonies

The Sinful Demand for Separateness

constitute his religion. But God and two men would be required for an object-lesson in Christianity. No man can show you what the Christian religion is until he has a Father whom he can love with all his heart, and with all his mind, and with all his strength, and a neighbor whom he can love as he loves himself.

The title that Jesus commonly used in speaking of Himself was The Son of Man. It was no robbery nor a prize to be grasped for Him to be on an equality with God, to be the Only Begotten Son of God. But in the first three Gospels almost a hundred times He calls Himself The Son of Man, and never once the Son of God. It would seem that He sought to more closely identify Himself with us by His designation of Himself to the end that He might say, not, "Give Me," as the Son of God, but, "Give us,"— the Son of Man speaking in common request with the sons of men. You remember the mutualism in His last prayer: "Father, glorify Thy Son that Thy Son may also glorify Thee." And then He looked upon His disciples and prayed, "Father, I will that they be with Me where I am, that the love wherewith Thou hast loved Me may be in them." He could not make request even in that sacred hour without including them and without lifting them up for a blessing, such as He prayed for Himself: "That they may be one as we are one, I in them and Thou in Me, that they may be one in Us."

The true aim of life is not a separate or closet saintliness, but a goodness that is of service in the concrete relations of husband and wife, parent and child, employer and employé, neighbor and citizen. Much of the best moral discipline we receive comes from the compulsory surrender of our selfish whims and caprices, and the consequent accommodation of ourselves to the rights of others, that is involved in being active, participating members of society. The highest achievement in Christian living is to become a normal and useful function in the organized life of men. In a mass of

The Sinful Demand for Separateness

iron dust, so long as each atom says, "Give me my separate place," the whole is useless. Once melted into unity and brought to the point where each atom is merged, with its fellows, into an iron bar, they all find their usefulness as the iron bar becomes the piston-rod turning the wheels of industry, or sings in the saw that turns out the lumber for a man's home. Nothing short of the union of one's personal interests with the interests of his fellowmen in the affairs of common life will secure the sort of character Jesus came to introduce. The organized man with social interests and social affections co-operating with other lives from whom he freely takes and to whom he freely gives, and with whom he accomplishes the great purposes of life, alone reveals the true glory of the individual.

As a consequence, union is not only strength, it is life. While I am physically alive, the different members and various atoms composing my body are held in organized unity. The eye does the seeing for itself and for the whole body, directing it in the way of safety and usefulness. The ears hear for the body, the feet walk for the body, and the mouth gives the body utterance. When death comes there is no longer this organized unity. The body separates and returns to the dust as it was. Separation is death, and death is separation. When your mind says, "Give me reading and study for my own sake," it too goes into a far country and wastes its substance. When your love nature is all turned within and expends itself upon itself, it is already beginning to be in want, and presently will be ready to fill itself with the husks the swine eat. To be separate anywhere is to be lost and dead. To be united with others in the common life is to be found and to be alive again.

On the physical plane, we all know that the single life is barren. It is only by the union of life with life that fruitfulness is attained. We are thus given a most significant hint. A man becomes his complete self

The Sinful Demand for Separateness

and helps to hand on life only through co-operation. And in the same way, if you detach yourself from family life, from society, from the life of the city, the state, the church, your efforts will become unfruitful; you will grow smaller and smaller until only a human speck remains, and at your death all vestige of your life will seem to vanish. The man who lives eternally is the man who completes himself by fellowship. To know the true God and to know the Son of Man, whom He has sent, by entering into the helpful service of the sons of men, is eternal life, and nothing short of that can be.

We see men all around us here who are living on a far-away island. They get the mail; they read the daily papers; they come and go without waiting for a sailing day. But in their isolation of sympathy and interest, in their separateness from the helpful activity of the community, in their insistent demand that they shall be let alone, they are lonely Crusoes, without even a man Friday to relieve the situation. The scientists have shown us the effect of such "island life." When Australia was cut off from the mainland, animal progress had not as yet reached the stage of mammals. And this great island, being separated from the current of advancement, developed nothing beyond marsupials. So when it was discovered, the only mammals found were a few rats, supposed to have come ashore from a sinking ship. Thus isolation and separateness in the mass or in the individual produce cases of arrested development.

We also see the penalty of separateness in the condition of the man who refuses to unite with the church. He sees that church membership entails obligations, some of them financial and social, others intellectual and moral. He declines these, and decides to remain outside. He may drop in and take a religious meal with you now and then, but he never finds his regular place at the table of the Lord. He

The Sinful Demand for Separateness

takes what portion of spiritual food he may lay hands upon, and carries it away to appropriate it alone. But he will soon spend all and begin to be in want. You will be apt to find him at last in some strange field, wishing he might satisfy his hunger by some unnatural food never intended for the soul of man. You regret that he did not come into some one of his Father's houses and find at His table bread enough and to spare. All these years he might have been serving Him as a son, and rejoicing in the fact that all that the Father hath is for the help of His children.

We see the bane of this selfish demand sometimes in the church itself. If some member in the secret of his own heart is habitually saying, "Give me my share of the offices, my portion of honor and attention;" if he is watching closely for slights, if he is waiting for people to bring him the portion of social goods that falleth to him, he is already on the borders of the far country. The only blessed way to live in the church is

Two Parables

to make the keynote of one's constant request, "Give us, as a church, the peace and joy, the strength and usefulness that falleth to us." The personal demand must be merged in a prayer for the general good. He that loses his life in striving for the general welfare, shall save it; and the man who keeps his life separate and jealously guards it, shall lose it.

That narrow conception of salvation where each man is making an unceasing and desperate struggle for his own eternal bliss, no longer appeals to men. Tertullian might picture the redeemed saints walking in the cool of the evening along the battlements of heaven, and being able from that safe vantage ground to see the suffering of the lost souls in hell. He might picture them singing additional praise to God, through the deeper sense of their own blessedness brought out by the sight of the contrast. But such a picture would simply disgust and repel the Christian congregation in a modern church. It is not the gross liter-

The Sinful Demand for Separateness

alness, but the immorality of it that offends the conscience of to-day. The first feeling in the hearts of the righteous, as we understand righteousness, would not be self-congratulation, but an impulse to organize a rescue mission. Unless there was a great and impassable gulf fixed, the righteous would spend their lives not in growing content, but in a sacrifice to bring help and deliverance to their unhappy fellows.

The seed of the separate, selfish, detached life must fall into the ground and die. If it die, it will bring forth the fruit of a social and serving nature. It will no longer seek to claim protected immunity from the burden and struggle of common life. It will count it all joy to become a loyal, hearty member of the social order. It will cast in its lot with its fellows, in an effort to make this world God's world, and to enable the children of men to live as the children of God.

The Hopefulness of a Sense of Need

"And he began to be in want."

The story is a miniature painting of our human experience. The race begins life in its Father's house when "heaven lies about us in our infancy." While we are children it can be said of us that of such is the Kingdom of Heaven. Then we gradually or suddenly take our portion of goods off into a far country and begin to live after the devices and desires of our own hearts. We waste the real substance of ourselves by disobedient living. Then there comes a time when we "begin to be in want." The animal food and the low companions of the far country are not enough. We long for our Father, and if we follow the line of the parable, we arise and go to Him with confessions on our lips and new purposes in our

The Hopefulness of a Sense of Need

hearts. The turning point with the young man, however, was when "he began to be in want." The discovery of an unsatisfied need was the first potent incentive to a better life.

The rude savage in the darkest part of Africa is probably more contented than any man or woman here to-day. He is more nearly satisfied with himself and with his situation than the richest or the most cultivated among you. He does not feel the unrest and ambition that troubles you. That is the sad fact in the case. He will make no progress until he is brought under the spell of discontent. But some teacher or some missionary comes upon him and, through precept and example, lifts before him a higher form of life. New ideas commence to get in on him, and he begins to be in want. He is blessed by "a presence that disturbs him" with the sight of higher things. He wants a shirt—he got on very well before unclad; but now his awakened sense of decency, and his better appreciation of adornment, demand clothing. Next he wants better facilities for cooking his food; then he wants a house; presently he wants a book, and then a Bible, and perhaps a Church. The growth and awakening of the man is indicated by this growing discovery of needs. When at last in every part of his nature he has learned to be in want, and when the essential needs of his human life are all demanding their appropriate satisfaction, then he is in the way of progress and of the attainment of his own completeness.

You find the same story in the unfolding of child-life. The history of the baby from soft, pulpy infancy, to sturdy, mature manhood, is the story of a constantly increasing discovery of needs. All the baby wanted at first was milk and a soft, warm place to sleep. Then he began to be in want of toys, simple, primitive, indestructible ones at first. He soon outgrew these and demanded amusement on a higher level. Then he wanted the companionship of his peers—

The Hopefulness of a Sense of Need

other children must be found to serve as playmates. Then he wanted pictures, then stories, then books. His ever-expanding needs gradually came to include games, exercise, teachers, society, the state, the church, at last a family of his own. Every year opened another mouth in some part of his life. He was constantly beginning to be in want of something more, to enable him to live his complete life; and his ever-increasing wants make up the story of his advance.

The Scriptures throughout recognize that "he began to be in want" is a most hopeful statement. Hunger is a sign of health, a prophecy of growth and strength. "Blessed are they that hunger and thirst after righteousness." Blessed are the men who feel empty and weak on account of their lack of goodness; the men whose mouths water at the sight of real righteousness; the men who have an inner gnawing and uneasiness prompting them to secure more of it! These are the men who "shall be filled." The "woe" is ever unto them that be "full;" the blessing is always upon those that are "in want."

Two men went up into the temple to pray. One of them was a Pharisee. He was not in want. He came in expressly to tell his Maker how well fed he was; how satisfied in respect to his righteousness. He reads off the bill of fare that he had gone through. He was not an extortioner, nor an adulterer, nor an unjust man, as some other men are; nor was he like that publican back there. He had fasted twice that week, and he had given a tenth of all he possessed. There was no hunger there, no want. He felt so full of righteousness that he would have refused another mouthful. The other man felt so empty, hungry, and mean, he could not stand up straight. He could not so much as look up or lift up his eyes unto heaven. He stood afar off and smote upon his breast and cried in his great need, "God be merciful to me, a sinner!" And the man in sore want went down to his

The Hopefulness of a Sense of Need

house justified rather than the other. Moral progress is always made by those who are in want, and not by those who feel that they are ethically well to do.

Want is everywhere a hopeful sign. St. Paul was passing through Athens. It had its three thousand gods, so that the wits claimed it was easier to find a god than a man. He felt his spirit stirred within him as he saw the city wholly given to idolatry. But presently he "found an altar with this inscription, TO THE UNKNOWN GOD." Here was an encouraging symptom! Here was touching evidence that certain souls did not find in any of the named and sculptured deities, the satisfaction for their need! There was still in Athens a hand reaching out empty; an eye peering into the darkness and not finding the object of its search; a heart unfed and crying for a god as yet "Unknown." If Athens was "in want" of some object of worship that it did not know, there was hope. Paul seized upon it for his text. He brought his bread of life to the place where he found an unfilled mouth. This God whom ye long for in ignorance, he cried, "Him declare I unto you."

When your physician comes to see you, he always asks at once, "How is your appetite?" If you have none at all, you are a sick man. If your appetite is uncertain, fitful, whimsical, and does not call for the right things, your body is out of order. An able-bodied, healthy man begins to be in want of good, wholesome food three times a day. That is one of the indications that he is in good health. That is also the first question the minister asks: Have you a good appetite? Do you hunger and thirst after righteousness? All healthy men do. Is your heart athirst for the living God? The souls of all men except those who are diseased, cry out for this communion with the Father. For all men and women who aim to live complete lives, righteousness is a necessity; religion is obligatory in the same way that food is

The Hopefulness of a Sense of Need

obligatory. The satisfactions to be found in religion are not thrust upon us by arbitrary command; they are demanded by our human nature when it is acting normally. Do you find that regularly you begin to be in want of the word of God, of the companionship of your Father, of the bread from His own table? If your appetite is keen, strong, natural, demanding the food that is needful for the life of a complete man, that fact is full of promise. But, if on the other hand you feel satisfied, or if your taste and palate are whimsical and love the unnatural, highly-seasoned things of worldliness and ungodliness, rather than the plainer fare of noble living, you are morally deranged.

The most discouraging sight we have to face is not that of some poor man with yearnings and longings that perhaps he will never be able to satisfy in this world. He may be living in a small house, wearing patched clothes, eating coarse food; but if he is a man hungry all the while for the real things of life, he is a merchant prince compared with the man who feels that he has already attained about all that heart can wish. In the book of Revelation, we are called upon to pity and to pray for a man whom the world does not often regard as pitiable. Our sympathy is asked for the one who says, "I am rich and increased with goods and have need of nothing." The last three words tell us in what a desperate, wretched state the man was. Need of nothing! If a boy feels that neither his father nor mother nor any of his elder friends can tell him anything, that he understands the situation perfectly, we are quite in despair over him. If a man reaches the point where he feels that he is "good enough" without the grace of God, and without the benefits that come through prayer and Christian service, we are distressed over the outlook for him. The most discouraging person here to-day is one whose habitual feeling is, "I have need of nothing."

The Hopefulness of a Sense of Need

When you go through the underground section of Chinatown, the saddest fact is not that our fellowmen are living there like rats in a hole; living so that the entire circle of wants can be met by a little cheap food, a narrow, dirty place to sleep, and a few low gratifications. The saddest fact is that they like it and are contented with it, and resist the attempts of the officers of the law to compel any change. They do not feel that they are in want. They are not pleading with the associated charities to come and rescue them. There is no Chinese cry for a sanitary commission to let in light and air. Their placid and stubborn satisfaction is one of the piteous elements in the situation. Indeed, the Chinese race is one of the most complacent of peoples. They can live on little and be content. Their very faces show it. It militates against their progress. The restlessness and discontent that mark the western races would be a hopeful symptom in the Chinese. If all those lives yonder in Chinatown could be roused so that they would begin to be in want of better food, more house room, more daylight and more fresh air, more books and pictures, more of everything that ministers to the total life, a shout of rejoicing would go up from all who are interested on their behalf!

The men who change the world are the hungry men; the agitating, inventive, revolutionary men; the men who cannot rest until they have sought to transform bad into good, and good into better, and better into best. Cæsar, with an eye to gathering the reins of government into his own great hands, and casting about for the possible sources of opposition, says:

> Let me have men about me that are fat:
> Sleek-headed men and such as sleep o' nights:
> Yond' Cassius has a lean and hungry look;
> He thinks too much: such men are dangerous.

However we may disapprove of the methods of the conspirators, if it were true that Rome was threatened with a military despotism, they were right in opposing it. And Cæsar was soundly correct in fearing

The Hopefulness of a Sense of Need

most of all the lean and hungry Cassius, who was "never at heart's ease." He was habitually in want. He was the restless leader of his party, desiring ever something better for Rome; desiring something better for himself than to be an underling with a military dictator striding over him. This restlessness made him dangerous to Cæsar, and would have made him useful to his brother men had his efforts been wisely directed to the betterment of the state.

The one hopeful thing about the many religious side-shows and the wide crop of mushroom growths of curious belief that infest all our cities, is that they indicate appetite. Here and there are little camps of people, most of them split off from the churches, holding and teaching views, some sound and wholesome, some merely odd and queer, and some openly in conflict with the words of our Lord! But these offshoots have sprung up because people were in want. Some one was hungry and insisted on the spreading of another table. There is a widespread feeling to-day that the indwelling spirit of God ought to have and can have a powerful influence on the health of the body. There is a growing conviction that a clear mind and a firm Christian faith have a distinctly therapeutic value; that "a sound heart is the life of the flesh." There is a feeling that many professing Christians do not enter into their full heritage as to spiritual experience and power. Men are claiming that there is open and possible to us something such as Jesus indicated when He spoke of "life more abundantly." And to the end that these claims and this expectancy may be met, there is a real demand that the interpretation of Scripture and the general presentation of religion shall be less mechanical and more vital.

All this growing appetite is hopeful. It is unfortunate that earnest and aspiring Christians sometimes split off and leave the organic Christianity of the community to become identified with irregular bands that mix queer and unscriptural notions with

The Hopefulness of a Sense of Need

some most helpful teachings. A steadfast adherence to the church of our Lord, and a deeper study of the Gospel there believed and there preached, would, I am confident, give to all these hungry, restless, separated lives bread enough and to spare, in their own Father's house. But the presence of this unrest and want in the community must be faced by the churches; its presence is prophetic of good; it ought to be welcomed and be led to find its satisfaction in the richer unfolding of the truth held already by the great Communion of Saints.

It is always a hopeful sign when any church begins to feel the stirrings of keener and stronger appetite. The only safety lies in its being perpetually in a state of want. You have seen, perchance, a church like this. The people had built for themselves a good house of worship, and paid for it. The pews were all let, and comfortably filled, each clear Sunday morning, with well-bred and agreeable people. The minister behaved well, was congenial socially, preached in an interesting way—and not too long at a time. There was a handsome legacy left by a departed wealthy member, so that the demands upon the generosity of the living were not severe. The seats, and, indeed, all the appointments of the church-life, were well cushioned, and now the members sat back and fanned themselves during "service" with great complacency!

And you know, without being told, how utterly and almost hopelessly dead and buried such a church is. The fine structure they have built to house their self-satisfaction, is a stately monument to the memory of the real life that departed, when they ceased to be "in want." A true church is unceasingly hungry. It is looking out for larger usefulness; it is eager and restless for deeper spiritual life and experience; it is athirst to satisfy itself by greater benevolence; it yearns to extend its usefulness to more lives, and to make deeper its impress for good, and to baptize the community more thoroughly with the sacred

The Hopefulness of a Sense of Need

blessedness with which it has been baptized.

One great object in preaching the Gospel is to open new mouths in men; to make them hungry for things which heretofore were not objects of desire. Human nature is more than a stomach to be filled or a back to be clothed. It is more than a nature to be amused or a mind to be stocked with news. It is all this, indeed, and these mouths should have their meat in due season. But in a complete account of human nature, we are not to forget that the central fact, the distinguishing characteristic of human life is the soul, the moral and spiritual nature. There is in man an ability to worship and pray and live to the full a religious life. If the mouths that demand such food have become closed, or if the appetite for it has fallen away, the case demands spiritual tonic and stimulus. The Gospel is to quicken and make the man restless and wistful, until he finds what will feed the deep, eternal part of him.

Two Parables

Lowell used to say that the business of education in its larger sense is to distribute, and to breed an appetite for, the real bread of life. The object of all the agencies in the community that make for civilization, that help to humanize men, is not only to put in the way of the hungry, seeking souls what they need, but also to awaken that desire in those who are going on without it. The college settlement moves down into the lower part of the city to teach the people new wants. It is not enough to send down tracts on cleanliness, industry, sobriety, politeness, and intelligence. The settlement must go down and plant a home there, that all these good words may come in the flesh and may dwell among the people, teaching them, by striking contrast, how much a clean house is to be preferred to a dirty one; how much better intelligence, sobriety, and politeness are than the opposites. The settlement shows, as nothing else could, how desirable are books and magazines, wholesome games and helpful

The Hopefulness of a Sense of Need

talk, good manners and good morals. It teaches the people to be hungry for these things by setting them all out in tempting array. When human desire is thus awakened, and is directed toward the right objects, it is well-nigh omnipotent, for it has God with it. If the nature and purpose of the universe be with our awakened aspirations, what can successfully stand against them? If it is the will of God in whom we live and move and have our being, that every normal mouth should have its meat in due season, shall not our total nature, when it feels and presents its wants, be fed from the fullness of Him that filleth all in all!

The same thing is true in matters of government. As we set before men higher ideals of national and municipal life, some taken from history, some from contemporary examples, some as reasonable conceptions of what is desirable, we awaken a hunger for a more honest, intelligent, economical, and effective administration of affairs. It is encouraging that so many writers and speakers on municipal reform, as well as many quiet citizens who give no public utterance to their feeling, are already in want. We have passed quite through the "hallelujah period" of our national life, when it was almost unpatriotic to suggest that anything American could be improved. We begin to realize that a government of the people, and by the people, and for the people, will not take care of itself any better than any other government. We are older, soberer, and wiser men, and many of the questions of administration are being taken up with a seriousness and determination that augurs well for the future. Men have begun to be in want of a better America, of better municipal government, and that want will continue to make itself heard until it is fed with what it demands.

The tremendous influence of a Christian civilization in awakening wants is seen in the widespread and resolute agitation along industrial lines. The workingmen are some-

The Hopefulness of a Sense of Need

times told they ought to be content; they have more comforts and more luxuries twice over than workingmen had two hundred years ago. There is no question about that. But the modern workingman wants more. His house must have more in it. He must read a daily paper. He and his family must have more of the things that make life livable, or he will be heard from. And the man is right. Christian civilization has come that he and that all men might have life, and might have it more abundantly. It is significant that this agitation is quite confined to Christian countries. India, China, Siam have no "labor movements" such as we find in Christian Europe and America. And in Protestant countries, England, Germany, and the United States, where the teachings of Jesus are in the hands of the common people, the pressure for social betterment is stronger than in Mexico, or Spain, or Italy. The men who company with Jesus and learn of Him, inevitably begin to be in want

Two Parables

and to insist that their needs shall be met.

Beware of those prosperous times when all needs seem to be fully satisfied! Success is often more perilous than failure. Keep the aspirations for something more, something higher, better, completer, ever awake. If the dullness and ease of satiety begin to creep upon you, pray to God that you may again feel the keen whip of unsatisfied desire. I hold before you this morning in the Gospel of Jesus Christ, in the privilege of Christian life and service, something that ought to be an object of desire to every one here. "Your Father knoweth what things ye have need of," and He has indicated your needs in the provision He has made. You have need of His grace; you have need of a Savior; you have need of the constant guidance of the Holy Spirit. You need all the help He offers for well-rounded and effective Christian living. May God abundantly feed all those whose hearts are already open, hungry and receptive! May

The Hopefulness of a Sense of Need

God help those who have not already found their way to the table of the Lord, to know their lack, and to feel an increasing unrest until they take the bread of God that cometh down from heaven to give complete life unto the world!

The Wisdom of Refusal

"And no man gave unto him."

It sounds almost heartless. The young man had wasted his substance until he had spent all. He began to be in want. He finally hired out to feed swine, but the job was so poor, he would fain have filled himself with the husks that the swine ate. And still, great as was his need, "no man gave unto him." The very next verse, however, tells us that at this point he came to himself, and remembered that in his father's house there was bread enough and to spare. He instantly resolved to arise, leave the far country, the swine, and the wicked life, and go to his father and begin to live once more as a son. The fact that men withheld their gifts while he was living wrong, is stated and is significant. If a

The Wisdom of Refusal

company of kind-hearted and good-looking women had gone out to the prodigal every day and left him a basket of delicacies to make his life there with the swine a little more comfortable, he might have been there yet. God intends that the way of the transgressor should be hard, and if you insist on making it soft, you encourage the transgressor to keep right on in it. The prodigal had no right to be living in a far country, feeding swine and hungry enough to eat husks. It was possible for him to be living as the son of his father, with bread enough and to spare. It served to remind him of all this, and to aid him in coming to himself, when "no man gave unto him."

Paul tells us not to be partakers of other men's sins. He indicates that we may become accomplices and parties to the wicked transaction by assisting men to be comfortable in their wrongdoing. If kind people will feed, and clothe, and pet some fellow who is living as the swine live, he will be a hundred-fold more ready to hold to that course than as though men withdrew their aid. Our course of action must be dictated by love, even toward the unthankful and the unjust. It must also be dictated by intelligence. What is meant for kindness must be, upon final analysis, really kind. There are times when the best shoulder to turn to a man is the cold shoulder. There are times when a man's greatest want is to go on being in want, and to find that no man will give unto him while he lives a bad life. It will render him an inestimable service in convincing him that he is on the wrong track. It will be your most forcible argument to persuade him to arise and be himself, and start for his Father's house.

> "We, ignorant of ourselves,
> Beg often our own harms which the wise powers
> Deny us for our good: so find we profit
> By losing of our prayers."

I may seem to you to be preaching hard-heartedness. Some people fancy that if we love men, it means we are to exhibit the same soft, weak, indulgent spirit toward

The Wisdom of Refusal

them, whether they do right or do wrong. We ought to learn a lesson from the quality and method of God's love toward us. God is love, infinite, absolute, unquenchable love. Yet with His own kind hands He has built the way of the transgressor so that it is hard and so that it will grow ever harder. A man in the museum of a medical school was looking at some specimens that showed the fearful results of certain physical sins. He turned to the physician and said, "Almighty God writes a very plain hand." Almighty God certainly does. "Behold, therefore, the goodness and the severity of God!" The harsh and terrible consequences that He visits upon broken law furnish the strong hint He gives men that they are going wrong. "He is kind unto the unthankful and to the evil;" and His refusal to make them, or even permit them to be comfortable in their iniquity, shows that His love is intelligently kind. "Be ye therefore merciful as your Father also is merciful."

Two Parables

There is a certain social ostracism which it is not only allowable but imperative for us to visit upon bold and contented wickedness. There are men "in society" who ought to be in jail. There are men whose smiling prosperity is the result of gambling. If good society tolerates and trains with them, when will they be taught to know the difference between the men who enter into the association of respectable people by the door, and the thieves and robbers who climb up some other way? Jesus would teach us to have the utmost charity for penitent wrongdoers, and when much is forgiven, there will be much answering love. But those brazen, self-satisfied, impudent sinners, who show their sleek and ugly heads in what is called good society, will have to learn their lesson as the prodigal learned his. If no man nor woman deigns to give them place or standing among decent people until there is a sober and persistent effort to make the life sufficiently decent to have its portion there,

The Wisdom of Refusal

the blessed Gospel will be effectively preached. Society has seen to it thoroughly that fallen women shall find that the way of such transgression is piteously hard. But in all such wicked transactions there are the supplementary fallen men, who need the same "vigor and rigor" in the message conveyed to them. A man with a dirty heart looks worse in society than a man with dirty hands or a dirty shirt, and he will do a thousand-fold more harm. If we insist so peremptorily that the outside of the cup and platter shall be clean, we should also demand a reputable degree of honesty and purity within.

I am sent into this pulpit to preach that we should love God and love men. But our love to men must be a love that really loves them. When the prodigal was there with the swine, hungry and empty, the man who might have rushed out to him and fed him and left him with the assurance that a loaf would be forthcoming every day, would not have loved him as much as the man who refused to give him a crust until he should get up and out and begin to make his life right. A wise refusal may be ten times more loving than a soft consent. Our good sense and our experience must choose the line of treatment that in the long run will prove loving. The surgeon who fearlessly cuts away a dangerous cancer even though his patient writhes, is more loving than the one who lets it grow and kill the man. Thou shalt love the Lord thy God with all thy heart, and with all thy soul, and with all thy *mind*, and with all thy *strength;* and thou shall love thy fellowman in the same four-fold way.

The principle suggested in the text is of special value in our charity work. There is a soft-heartedness that deals out provisions at the back door, and hands over money to the able-bodied beggar who stops you on the street, which does more harm than good. This human nature of ours is prone to be lazy, and some of it is very lazy. When an easy-going man finds that it is

The Wisdom of Refusal

easier to beg than to work, it is a fatal discovery, and his choice is soon made. What he needs is not alms, but to make several more trips to the ant and to give additional consideration to her ways, in that without the spur of guide, overseer, or ruler, she diligently provides her meat in the summer, and gathers her food in the harvest. "Blessed is the man who *considers* the poor" as well as gives them alms. Blessed is the man who reaches into his intelligence and into the combined wisdom and experience of charity workers, at the same time that he reaches into his pocket.

In the city of Boston, a few years ago, a royal-hearted young man, an earnest Christian worker in one of our churches there, felt that he could do something for the unemployed. He rented a large basement, fitted it up with cots, with a reading-room, and a place for Gospel meetings. It would hold one hundred and fifty men. He went to the hotels and got their broken bread for little or nothing; he got their coffee-grounds; he bought beans at a low price; and he found he could give a man all the bread he could eat, a half pint of beans, a cup of coffee, and a night's lodging, all for ten cents. It seemed very philanthropic. A Gospel meeting was held each evening, and the superintendent of this mission, whose theology would have made Jonathan Edwards seem a trifle liberal in comparison, preached them a red-hot sermon. The tramps all over eastern Massachusetts, and some in New Hampshire and Vermont, heard of it and came down to put up with our friend for the winter. They found that by a little persistent effort they could beg ten cents on the Common in an hour or so, and then go down to the mission, pay for their keep, and spend the remainder of the twenty-four hours as gentlemen of leisure. The reading-room and the checker-boards helped them to pass the time. The evening sermon was an inexorable condition and was exceedingly robust, but they did not mind. They felt that every situation in

The Wisdom of Refusal

life has its outs. The city of Boston was calling for more men to shovel snow on the streets at the very time the brethren of the easy chair were dozing in this mission. It was all well meant, but in most of the cases it was mistaken kindness. The tenderest thing that could have been done for any able-bodied man would have been for no man to give unto him, and to thus compel him to a self-respecting life of honest work.

It was Herbert Spencer who said, "To save men from the consequences of their folly is to fill the world with fools." The same is true where there is a lack of thrift or sobriety. Make any sort of wrong living easy and comfortable, and you send out a bid for men to enter in and enjoy the results of their folly. If you coddle and pet the transgressor instead of leaving him where the Bible leaves him, you put a premium on transgression. "The tender mercies of the wicked are cruel," and so is the ill-directed kindness of some of the righteous. When we are dealing with men who are wantonly breaking the law of prosperity or the moral law, we shall do well to remember that "the injuries that they themselves procure must be their schoolmasters." For us in our mistaken mercy to relieve them from the results of their own sin, is turning them out of the very school whose lessons they sorely need.

All this is said with a full understanding of the fact that misfortunes come which men cannot avert; that it is oftentimes difficult for the incompetent to find work, and that in every community there are the "deserving poor." But the worst enemies the deserving poor have are the lazy impostors, who break down the confidence of benevolent people; these men who only lack ten cents to make up the fare to Stockton or Fresno; these unfortunates who have just had their pockets picked and want to borrow a few dollars to get back to their families at Sacramento, when they will instantly mail the money back to you. There may be exceptions, but most of them are

The Wisdom of Refusal

liars and thieves. All city pastors are visited by such men who frequently claim to be Christian Endeavorers, and deacons, and some of them brother ministers; and who want to negotiate a small loan on the strength of these spiritual bonds. Sometimes they abuse us roundly for our hard-hearted incredulity when we refuse them! The whole tribe of them is bringing reproach upon those who are worthy of our aid. Faithful are the wounds which their real friends inflict upon them by wise refusals, but the financial kisses of their enemies are deceitful. The only proper answer is that suggested in the text—"Let no man give unto them."

In every community there are the aged, the sick, and the helpless whom we ought to help. Christ, by His example and by His words, laid this duty upon us. But careful statistics have shown us that out of every ten persons applying for help, in six cases the want is due to intemperance; in three, it is on account of helpless old age, or broken down condition, following upon a wasteful or reckless life; and there is left one case of actual, deserving necessity. Edward Everett Hale, one of the most experienced men in charity work, was accustomed to say that if the other churches in Boston would take care of the poverty caused by drink, he and his church would care for all the rest. If a man is led to feel confident that he can spend half his wages or all of them on rum, and that the community will then step in and support his wife and children, it is not a good temperance lesson for him. But the cry is, "The poor woman ought not to suffer." The poor woman is responsible for being his wife. The man and the woman are responsible for the presence of the children. The lifting off from people's shoulders of the consequences of their own acts will not tend to make them wiser and better. I hope the poor women will go on suffering from drunken husbands until they learn while they are girls not to marry habitual

The Wisdom of Refusal

drinkers. With so many lines of employment open, no girl needs to marry for support. Marriage is not a necessity. It is the happiest way to live, but only when it is marriage of the right sort. When we are compelled to face and to bear the natural consequences of our own choices, we receive moral education of the most effective kind.

Out in the natural world there goes on a stern weeding out of forms of life that will not conform to certain laws. The survival of those who are fit to survive results from the struggle for existence laid upon plants, upon animals, and upon men. Laid on by whose hand? The natural world was not created by the devil. God the Father Almighty is Maker of heaven and of earth. The stern struggle for existence was imposed by the God of all grace. To step in and remove it by making it easy for the drunken, and the lazy, and the shiftless forms of life to survive, is a charity against nature. When certain individuals take up with a form of life that is described by saying it is in a far country, it is down with the swine, and it wastes its substance with harlots, the only right course is for no man to give unto it. Let it begin to be in want and remain in want until it comes to itself and leaves that pigsty mode of life! Starve it until from dire necessity it arises and starts for the place where there is bread enough, a Father's house and a Father's love, and all the other rewards of righteousness!

Applying the text in a different direction, no man should give anything to sustain an institution which has no rightful place in a Christian civilization. The workingman who gets twelve dollars a week, on Saturday night, as Dr. Gladden has well said, "has power over all men to the extent of twelve dollars." He can choose where his power will be exercised. Wherever he spends his money, he sets men at work producing the thing he buys. If he spends it for flour, meat, fruit, furniture, or books, he stimulates the production of

The Wisdom of Refusal

these good things. If he spends it, or any part of it, for whisky and beer, he starts more men in the rum business. A man who gambles or sinks himself in lower indulgences, increases the demand for gamblers and outcasts. If he buys a bad book or a bad picture, or indulges in low, cheap forms of amusement, he increases the demand for that sort of thing, and makes it a more profitable line of business. As the dollar leaves your hand, in any direction, it sets men to work furnishing the thing you buy. You become partaker of other men's sins when you share in maintaining what has no rightful place in a Christian civilization.

The notorious prize fight at Carson City last March, including the purses, admissions, traveling expenses, and the liquor consumed in making the fight go off well, is said to have cost something over seventy-five thousand dollars. Enough to have erected a public library in some city, a thing of blessing and benefit for generations to come! Enough to have built a workingmen's club, with bathrooms, reading rooms, recreation rooms, meeting rooms, all complete! All spent for the sake of seeing, in a few minutes, which of two men could most successfully bruise and disfigure the face of his fellowman. Where did they get so much money? From the great number of men who paid the admissions and spent their means. Prize-fighters furnish fights because there is a demand for them. Newspapers devote the first and best pages next morning to the disgraceful occurrence because people want to read the details of every round. The people who demand it and patronize it are responsible. The only way to get rid of such things is for no man to give unto them.

The majority of our city newspapers at this time are sensational, unclean, and unreliable. But they furnish what people buy. If the people would not buy a paper with startling headlines and abominable pictures, and pages of low talk concerning some

The Wisdom of Refusal

scandal, the paper would no more print it than they would print a chapter from Rollin's Ancient History. The only way to stamp out a bad paper is for no decent man to support it by subscription or advertisement. If the decent people insist on taking, and reading, and advertising in the best paper, the best paper will flourish and grow still better. The decent people in this community, or in any large community, outnumber the indecent people ten to one. They could have their way and could have it all the time, if they would simply act together.

The responsibility in spending our money is thus as great and as sacred as our responsibility in earning it. Both must be done in a way that tends to build a Christian civilization. The sweating system results from the greed of manufacturers, and also from the popular demand for cheap clothing. Men will only make what people are ready and eager to buy. We all know that about a certain amount is a fair price for a suit of clothes or for a shirt. When we refuse to pay that fair price and begin to run after unreasonable bargains, and to buy at prices that mean starvation wages for the women and girls who do the work, we are accomplices in the whole wretched business of sweating. To turn away from the bargain counters and from certain stores may mean a stricter economy for us; it may mean that we shall need to follow the fashions afar off, but we shall not be implicated in building up an industry that is ruinous to the poor, tired hands and brains engaged in it.

The question of popular amusements often agitates the church people. No doubt there could be in every city decent and wholesome theaters; so wholesome that a minister could go with no more discredit to his calling than there is in his going to a symphony concert, or in taking dinner with one of his deacons. It could be as profitable for me to go and see Shakespeare's plays on the stage as to sit in my study

The Wisdom of Refusal

and read them—more profitable, for they were written to be acted more than to be read. But that day has not yet come. The modern theaters too commonly offer performances where women and girls appear in costumes that cannot but be destructive to the modesty and finer feelings of those participating. The delicacy and modesty of the woman on one side the footlights is as much worth preserving as that of the woman on the other. That the tendency of the stage, as at present conducted, is deleterious, is indicated by the claim that Mrs. Kendall, the English actress, made a few years ago, to the effect that she was the only virtuous woman on the English stage. Her claim was disputed, with reason, no doubt; and she was severely criticised for such an assertion. But the very possibility of such claim ever being made with any sort of ground to make it appear credible, indicates the situation. Imagine a woman who was a teacher, or a dressmaker, or engaged in domestic service,

Two Parables

making such a ridiculous claim touching her fellow-craftsmen! But if the stage destroys modesty and tends to destroy virtue, the people who sustain it are responsible equally with those who furnish the performance. The way to usher in the better day is not to consume all our zeal denouncing the theater managers, who simply furnish what people will buy. The decent, modest, high-minded people must simply refuse to patronize any performance that interferes with the modesty and high-mindedness of those participating. If we give our support only to forms of recreation that are pure, lovely, and of good report, we shall help to starve out those that are unworthy, and to introduce those that can rightfully claim a place in Christian society.

The modern schools of physical well-being teach us to maintain health less by the use of violent drugs than by correct diet and wholesome exercise. If there is too much of something in the body, we do not go on putting in more; we starve the

The Wisdom of Refusal

body as to that and feed it the other elements. If the body is sore with boils, we cut off the food of which boils are made and supply another sort. The same common-sense treatment is good for the social and industrial body. Let no man give a farthing to a form of life or an institution that has no rightful place in the body of Christian civilization. The responsibility for the presence of the sores and morbid growths must lie with all who are supporting them. When this rigorous policy of refusing the sinews of war to all enemies of our social peace is strictly pursued, there will be some hope that society will come to itself and arise and enter upon a better mode of life.

The same principle applies to the individual life. There may be an element in you that habitually goes into a far country and spends itself in wrong thinking, wrong desiring, and wrong doing. If you make it comfortable for that prodigal element, it will stay. If you sternly and stubbornly

Two Parables

starve it, inevitably it must come to itself and cast in its lot with your better self, and come at last with your total nature to the Father. An ugly temper grows by indulgence, or dies for lack of sustenance. Impure thoughts and desires grow impudent and masterful by being allowed their daily ration of food; they wither and die when they are denied. Selfishness becomes a hateful usurper, demanding the whole field if allowed to feed daily at the table of our allowance; but if compelled to become an ascetic, denying itself, taking up its cross and following Christ in active service, it puts off the old man and puts on a new man of unselfish love.

Christian Science scores a point of strength by insisting that people shall starve the evil and feed the good. It discourages you from talking of your ailments. They do not form an interesting or profitable topic for others. They are not profitable to the man himself, though they must be interesting, for some people seem

The Wisdom of Refusal

to "enjoy poor health." Christian Science carries this starvation of evil so far as to deny its very existence. There its extravagant philosophy breaks down into absurdity. If I cannot trust the integrity of my consciousness when it informs me that I have the toothache, how am I to believe it when it tells me I am in health, or that I love God? But a stubborn and persistent refusal to think upon or talk about one's ills will, indeed, tend to starve them out, and will have a real therapeutic effect. To feed the mind and heart upon thoughts of health and strength, will enable the healing process of nature and of scientific treatment to do their best.

One fine point in this parable, also, is the way it shows how the whole constitution of things changes for a man when he is changed himself. When the prodigal was spending his all in the far country, wasting his substance with harlots and hungry enough to fill himself with husks, "no man gave unto him." When he arose, went to his father with a confession, and entered upon a new life, his father had compassion and ran and fell on his neck and kissed him. The servants brought out a robe, and a ring, and shoes. They killed the fatted calf and all began to be merry. A new man finds a new world ready to his hand. God and society, and the whole system of things, refuse to give their good gifts while the man lives wrong. They all unite in their welcome and their encouraging help when he faces about.

As you give to charity, then, as you spend your money, as you select your forms of recreation, as you bestow time, thought, and care on the various parts of your own life, see that they all go to maintain something that has a right to be. By exercising the wisdom of refusal, starve out the wicked and prodigal elements in society and in yourself, and then feed the mouths that are normal and healthy with "that meat which endureth unto everlasting life, which the Son of Man shall give unto you."

The Naturalness of a Religious Life

"When he came to himself, he said, ... I will arise and go to my father."

That was the natural thing for him to do. The normal place for a Hebrew boy was in his father's house and at his father's table, rather than away in a pagan country herding swine for a Gentile. He seemed, as he sat there, to have awakened to the fact that it was strange and unnatural for him not to be with his father. He saw how irrational and absurd it was for him to be hungry enough to eat husks, when there was bread enough and to spare in his own father's house. And when he thus came to himself, he came at once to his father.

When a man is under the influence of liquor, we say, "He is not himself." We do not stop to say or to think who he is—he is not the man we know. Some foreign element has gotten into him, and for the time usurps the place of the man who is naturally resident there. If a man loses his temper and does foolish, cruel deeds, we say, "He is not himself." If a man's reason is dethroned and he becomes insane, we say, "He is not himself." You see how these familiar expressions all bear testimony to the fact that we believe that a real man is sober, kind, and reasonable. The fundamental, unmixed human nature is good; when it becomes anything else, the man is not himself.

Sin is always abnormal; righteousness alone is normal. A sinner of a certain sort in the Old Testament was called "a strange woman." All wickedness is strange. It is a foreign immigrant that has never become naturalized. It never can become naturalized in the kingdom of humanity, for it cannot take the oath of allegiance. It has none of the possibilities of loyal citizenship within it. No matter what form the sin takes, we insist that it is

The Naturalness of a Religious Life

an interloper, a squatter in the domain of the man's real nature. It does not belong there; it has no title to its place. It is pre-empting soil that was created for holy uses. The sinning man is a false self posing in the place of the true self. The real man may be temporarily overpowered by liquor, by evil temper, by the infatuation of some wicked companion; in every case we insist that he is not himself. Underneath there is another man, the real man, who is sober, kind, and pure. Salvation, then, is in reality self-recovery. The restoration and the redemption of the man consist in his being brought thoroughly and eternally to himself.

The Bible, from the very first, bids us cherish this truth. Man was created in the likeness and image of God. The first sin was the act of introducing something into man's life that did not belong there. Human nature is termed in the teaching of Jesus, a field, sown in the first instance with good seed by the Son of Man. The tares that subsequently appeared were corruptions, introduced, the parable says, by "an enemy." You may stoop down to the beginning of human life, as Jesus did, and hold it up, saying, "Of such is the Kingdom of Heaven." The mature man may or may not belong in that kingdom. If he has introduced into his life any sinful element, then he is no longer himself. And when once he has brought in those sinful elements, which we find to be the universal fact, they must be washed out by repentance and faith in the blood of Jesus Christ. "Except ye turn and become as little children, ye shall in no wise enter the Kingdom of Heaven."

You can see the whole spiritual process taking place there in the prodigal's heart. He was foolish at first in leaving his father's house. He foolishly spent his time and his money in riotous living. He wasted his substance, his health, his good name with harlots. He plunged into dissipation until he began to be in want.

The Naturalness of a Religious Life

Then at last, there in the quiet of the field, where he was herding swine, he began to see things as they are. He saw how ugly were the cruel and painted faces for whose false smiles he had been wasting his money and his life. He saw how treacherous were the men who had caroused with him until "he had spent all," and then had left him to the swine. The whole situation where he had found himself was strange, foreign, unnatural. He thought of his life at his father's house; it had been sweet, pure, simple. He gradually awoke out of what seemed like an ugly, wicked dream; he came to himself and quickly announced his determination, "I will arise and go to my father."

A Christian man always is one who has had his eyes opened and who is trying to be himself. He will not be some twisted, contorted, unnatural caricature—he will be himself. He will be the man God made him to be. When we speak of a man who is notoriously cruel, we call him "inhuman." All sin is inhuman. To be human is to be Christian; it is to do the things that a human life was created to do. The best account any man can give as to his reasons for living a religious life is to simply say, "I am religious because I am a man and do not desire to be less than human, and because humanity in me and in my race commences and completes itself in religion and by religion." A Christian man worships and prays; he was intended to do that. He would be queer and unnatural if he did not. A boy who never speaks to his father, we call a morbid and unnatural boy. A man who does not speak to his Heavenly Father is not himself. A Christian obeys the will of God. He was made to do just that. A disobedient man is a planet out of its orbit, plunging wildly through space, certain to bring and to suffer disaster. A Christian man, by the grace of God, keeps himself kind, true, pure. An unkind, false, impure man is always an adulterated article. In a word, when a

The Naturalness of a Religious Life

man becomes a Christian he is not introducing some foreign substance into his nature; he is simply bringing out the original purpose. Religion is not something added to life; it is life itself. The true nature of the man when freed by the forgiveness and grace of God from the hindering and corrupting elements in it, is in itself Christian character. So when a man arises and goes to his Father, he is on the way to become completely and eternally himself.

Amiel says that we are "candidates for humanity." We have not all, as yet, made our calling and election to that high destiny sure. Indeed, the aim of education, of culture, and of religion is to humanize men. All right life tends to bring the human nature to the point where it is entirely itself. And one of the glories of Christianity is that it has brought in a new conception of what it is for a man to be himself. A North American Indian would give one answer if you were to ask him to describe the natural life. The negro slave at the close of the war would have given another. A white man a thousand years ago would have given still another. A wicked man in the slums at this hour would give you yet another, if you should ask him to define his notion of the natural life. A Christian man goes for his conception of the natural life to the complete man, the representative man, the Son of Man. For a man to be himself is for him to be like Jesus Christ. Untainted, uncorrupted humanity appeared to us in the life of the Savior, and for all time we can truly realize what it means to be human. To be a man means to "be like Him," ever increasing in our power to adequately "see Him," and then to reproduce Him, "as He is."

The strangeness of the religious life has been mistakenly emphasized by some teachers. They have overworked and distorted the idea that we are to be "a peculiar people." The revised version trans-

The Naturalness of a Religious Life

lates it "a people for God's own possession." The revision and correct translation of all texts and all facts will make it clear that it is the unchristian life that is odd and strange. When that passage in Corinthians is rightly translated, it is no longer a slant at human nature. We find that it is not "the natural man," but "the sensuous" or "animal man" that "receiveth not the things of the spirit of God." The more natural the life becomes, the more Christian it will be. Jesus sought always to emphasize the fact that the Christian life is the inevitable life for one who would be a normal man. The lost sheep and the lost coin and the prodigal son are in the strange and unnatural position. The favorite method of Jesus throughout was to show the close affinity between human nature acting healthfully and the nature of God. When He desired to illustrate the gracious answers that God sends to our prayers, His word was, "What man is there of you, whom if his son ask bread, will he give him a stone?" And the truth that God must inevitably come into the world to seek and to save that which is lost is foreshadowed, Jesus said, in the familiar fact that if a man have a hundred sheep and one be gone astray, he leaves the ninety and nine, and goeth into the mountains and seeketh the one until he find it. He sought to justify the ways of God to men by uncovering and interpreting the resemblances between human life at its best and the perfect life of God. His method of teaching deepened our sense of the fact that when human nature is pure and normal, it is indeed a finite image and likeness of the Divine.

Take the conception of the entrance upon a new life put forth in the text. How wholesome and natural it all is! It is the act of rising and of going to one's Father. What a helpful way of putting it! The words form a well that is deep, and you may drink as you will of their living water and never exhaust them. In our knowl-

The Naturalness of a Religious Life

edge of human fatherhood, we have something to draw with. Any child knows what it means to arise and go to his father. There on the hills of Judea, when Jesus spoke, and here in Oakland to-day you find fathers toiling for their little ones. Men are working to give their children comfortable homes, a good education— better than they themselves had — and something to start them in the world. The whole aim of fatherhood is to help the children to a successful career, to a good name, and to a bright destiny. That is fatherhood as you know it and see it. Now enlarge your thought of it! Take from it all imperfectness of knowledge, all lack of power! Deepen it, widen it until it is as broad as from the east to the west! Lift it until it is as high as the heaven is above the earth! Make your fatherhood perfect, absolute, infinite, and you know what to think of God! To live a Christian life is to arise and go to Him, and cast in your lot with Him! Religion, Jesus said, is

Two Parables

summed up in this: It is doing the will of that Father who is in heaven by the constant help revealed and brought to us through His only Begotten Son, our Savior.

When we would understand the meaning of any doctrine or of any problem, we shall succeed best if we arise and go to the Father and examine it in the light of this fundamental truth as to the Fatherhood of God. Jesus was accustomed to translate His doctrines into the terms of human life, to the end that they might the better feed and bless men. Now, no man hath seen God at any time, but he that hath seen Jesus hath seen the Father. Suppose we should hold up some of the truths of religion and read them in the light of this parable, which is called "the parable of the prodigal son," but which is still more "the parable of the Father." Let us ask each doctrine to arise and go to the Father and uncover its meaning in His presence!

What is sin? It is the act of a child saying, "Give me my portion of goods," and

The Naturalness of a Religious Life

then taking his ability, his time, and his money off into a far country to spend them for selfish gratification.

What is repentance? It is the act of a child, away from home, beginning to be in want, surrounded with food that feeds animals but does not feed men, who comes at last to himself and says, I will arise and go to my Father.

What is atonement? It is what a parent suffers because of his child's sin. It is the painful sacrifice a Father makes in going down into the sinful situation where his children are entangled, in order to win them back to righteousness. It is the act of a Father seeing his son a great way off and going out to meet him and to bring him home. It is the vicarious suffering endured when "God was in Christ reconciling the world unto Himself."

What is grace? It is a beautiful name for the way a father helps his children to live right. Suppose one of you that is a father had a son who had become a drunkard. He reeled through the streets and disgraced you. He broke your heart and left your home. Suppose he came to himself and came home, saying, "I have done wrong; I want to live a new life; I am not worthy to be your son, but give me a place in the store that I may earn an honest living." You know what you would do. You would give him the place; you would also take him into your home and into your heart. If, on some dark night, he told you that he must go down town on an errand, and that he feared to pass the saloon doors lest the old appetite should master him, you would not suffer him to go alone. You would walk down beside him; and if his arm should tremble as the fumes of liquor were wafted out from some door of temptation, you would simply draw him more closely to you, steadying him, assuring him of a deeper love, and thus walk on with your son. That is grace! If any one of you that is a father knows how to help his faulty children, how much more compas-

The Naturalness of a Religious Life

sion does your Heavenly Father feel for those who need Him.

What is worship? It is the act of a child associating with his Father; loving to be where He is; entering by all the ways that have become sacred and dear into His closest companionship; loving this all the more because he is surrounded by the other children. "True worshipers shall worship the *Father* in spirit and in truth, for the Father seeketh such to worship Him."

What is prayer? "When ye pray, say Our Father." Prayer is the act of a child speaking to his Father. You see how natural, how rational prayer is. How morbid and queer a man is who never prays!

What is duty? It is the loving compulsion from within that a son feels when he says, "I must be about my Father's business." It is the choice of a son who remains with his Father, asking for nothing better than to do His will and to share His work, and who presently hears his Father say, "Son, thou art ever with Me, and all that I have is thine."

What is assurance? You remember Paul's text, "I know whom I have believed, and I am persuaded that he is able to keep that which I have committed unto him." But the words of Jesus are even better. Assurance is the feeling of security and protection that the children of God enjoy because they have placed their lives unreservedly in His hands. They look up and out in quiet confidence saying, "No man is able to pluck them out of my Father's hand."

What is death? When a child is weak, sick, tired, no longer able to stand physically, and when he falls back into his Father's arms, he naturally says, "Father, into Thy hands I commend my spirit." For every Christian, death should properly be an act, and that act is the experience of death.

What is immortality? It is the fact that children will naturally share in the same

The Naturalness of a Religious Life

blessed and endless life of their Father. When they are doing His will and knowing His love, they see Him bending toward them, and they hear His voice calling to them, "Because I live, ye shall live also."

We might box the whole compass of religion, and be guided unerringly by the fact that the true magnetic needle will point ever to the cardinal truth of the Divine Fatherhood. But from these illustrations, you get the method. In the interpretation of any doctrine, in attempting to know the meaning of any duty or burden, in solving any mystery in religion, it is good to arise and go to the Father and construe all things by this fundamental fact, that "to us there is but one God, the Father."

Men have sometimes been afraid to state or to believe in the Fatherhood of God in such unhesitating fashion. It is urged that sinful men will presume upon it. It seems risky, they say, to put forth this conception of God so boldly and baldly. A sufficient answer would be to cite the example of Jesus. His pupils have taught the Fatherhood of God, but none of them so fully as did the Master. Other Bible writers called God the Father, but not one of them so many times as did Jesus Himself. We are entirely safe in following this example of our Lord.

But if we should desire to preach the sovereignty of God, there is no sovereignty to be preached like that of the Father. Suppose that I should steal. The law of California would seize me. The sovereignty of this state would send me to prison. But the severity of all that would not occasion my keenest suffering. The stone walls, the iron bars, the hated stripes, the bread and water—I could bear all these. Other men have hardened themselves against them—I could. I should suffer most because of the pain I should bring to my father. Yonder in that old home, the thought of his broken heart, of the utter disappointment of all his fond hopes, of his tears of grief over the sad fact that all his sacrifice and

The Naturalness of a Religious Life

anticipation on my behalf had come to this—that would bring my keenest pain. The knowledge of my base ingratitude to the kind hearts that cared for me in childhood would be a keen lash that would beat me with many stripes. That thought would be stronger to deter me from wrongdoing than the thought of the sternest prison. The vision of the sovereignty of California justice, strictly and sternly administered, would not begin to hold the restraining power contained in the sight of my father's love. It is an awful thing for men to lie or swear, to be impure or selfish or ungodly—because God is their Father. Arise and go to your Father, if you would know how black sin is, and if you would learn the strongest motive for hating unrighteousness.

The terrible attitude of God toward wrongdoing cannot be stated more strongly than to say, He is "the Father." God hates sin with an awful hatred because it hurts men. It hurts His children. If any one of you that is a father should find some night that an ugly brute had broken into your home with a wicked purpose toward your daughter, whose indignation would be most terrible? Whose right arm would strike the hardest blow? Not the policeman's, not the judge's, not the reformer's—but the right arm of the father!

Those who would suggest that preaching the Fatherhood of God incessantly as Jesus did, will lead men to feel that God is a soft, indifferent, easy-going Being, who scarcely knows right from wrong, and who treats all men alike, whether they work righteousness or work iniquity, do not understand the meaning of fatherhood. I have asked you this morning to read the beautiful promises about grace, prayer, and forgiveness, with the word Father in your hand. Read the solemn and severe passages in the same way. You will not be able to pronounce the words or get their meaning unless you do. God is a consuming fire. God is angry with the wicked

The Naturalness of a Religious Life

every day. The wicked shall be turned into hell, and all the nations that forget God. We learn the meaning of this attitude toward iniquity when we find that it is the feeling of a father against the evil that would destroy his child. There is no wrath like the wrath of the Lamb, the indignation of self-sacrificing love against the enemies of its redemptive passion.

This method of interpreting Scripture and doctrine in the light of our Father's presence brings out, as no other method can, the naturalness and the essentialness of the Christian life. Salvation no longer lies in our minds as a question of securing or not securing certain outward joys and comforts in this world and in the world to come. The matter of salvation is the question as to whether a man will be himself or lose himself. We must ask, "What distorted caricature would a man be willing to receive in exchange for himself?" The healthy, normal, and well-rounded human life can be no other than the Christian life. If any man would come completely and finally to himself, he must of necessity arise and go to his Father.

It is good to remember, also, in this connection what appears to have been the efficient cause in bringing the prodigal to this new determination. The discomforts of his environment are named, but the controlling motive seems to have come from the fact that he remembered he had a father. It is regarded as good form in some quarters to-day to utter slants at theology. Culture is put to the fore, and in the emphasis laid upon the wholesomeness and naturalness of the ethical life, the supernatural is wellnigh crowded out. In the face of such a contention, it is reassuring to notice that in this intensely human parable it was theology that put the prodigal in the way of salvation. The thought that he had a father; the knowledge that in that far-away father's house there was bread enough and to spare; the confidence that a return and a confession would establish him, at least,

The Naturalness of a Religious Life

upon the footing of a hired servant in that house of plenty—these were the considerations that started him upon a new life. For the moral betterment of the world, it is not less theology we need, but more and better theology. Men will never be able to make this earth what it ought to be until they see that it has a heaven above it; nor can they themselves become what they ought to be until they learn to look for direction and assistance up to Almighty God. It will be good to phrase this theology as Jesus phrased it, in terms of human life rather than in the dialectics of the schoolmen. Our statements of doctrine in order to enter the closed doors, and to be able to open men's understandings and to effectively say, " Peace be unto you," must not be disembodied, abstract theories; they must have flesh and bones. And in this translation of the Gospel message into a tongue wherein all men were born, we shall be guided aright if we become as little children, and do always behold "the face of the Father who is in heaven." We shall be enabled to set before men the reasonableness and the naturalness of the religious life, and we shall come to be our complete selves, just in proportion as we arise and go to that Father.

A Personal Confession

"I have sinned against heaven and before thee."

That was the first thing the prodigal said when he came back to his father. It is the first thing any man says when he really decides to live a new life. The young man was away in a far country, living wickedly. When he came to himself, he said, I will arise and go to my father, and my first statement in his presence will be a personal confession of my own fault—"I have sinned." The moment he resolved to go back and stand before his father and say that, he was in the way of becoming a better man. The personal acknowledgment of guilt, coupled with the personal utterance of a desire for forgiveness, lies at the very threshold of a new life. It is a door, and any man who enters by that door, into the presence of Jesus Christ, will be saved.

It is not the way men often try to begin new lives. It is common when we have done wrong to offer first a string of excuses. The prodigal could have read his father a list of "extenuating circumstances:" "The harlots tempted me." "I was young, and evil companions led me astray." "My father made a great mistake in putting into my inexperienced hands the portion of of goods that fell to me." A bad man who wants an excuse for being bad will always find one that will be satisfactory to those who are satisfied with it. But there was none of this in the returning prodigal. He stood right out in the open, and frankly acknowledged his fault like a man, "I have sinned." The story would never have ended with a robe and a ring and a kiss of acceptance, if he had begun in any other way. A series of lying excuses will never prove a lamp unto a man's feet nor a light unto his path to

A Personal Confession

guide him in the way of moral peace and strength.

Moral cowardice dates away back. We find it appearing in the very first instance of wrongdoing. When Adam was called to account for eating the forbidden fruit, he turned around and laid the blame on his wife—"The woman gave me and I did eat." Then the woman passed it on by laying the fault at the door of the devil—"The serpent tempted me and I did eat." The author does not follow it any further; no doubt, if the serpent had been interviewed, he would have passed the blame along, too. You find the world began with this same lazy, cowardly unwillingness to acknowledge guilt. Who can say how the story of the Garden of Eden would have ended, if, instead of excusing himself by blaming others, Adam had fallen in penitence before the Almighty, saying, "I have sinned." We do know that when the prodigal came back from his wrongdoing with that confession on his lips, he was joyfully restored to his father's house and his father's heart. Men are always turned out of the garden of happiness when they blame others for their own sin; they are faced at once toward the best robe and the best food and the highest joy when they forsake their wrongdoing and go to their Father with personal confessions on their lips.

A mother in her mistaken kindness may always find excuse for the faults of her children. The teachers are to blame because they do not like their Sunday-school; the public school teachers are at fault because the children do not learn more nor behave better; those uncouth playmates have made her darlings rude and quarrelsome. These soft excuses are offered in the presence of the children until they become self-righteous little prigs, imagining that, undisturbed by outside influence, they never could go wrong. Being relieved of blame, they gradually lose the definite moral sense; they come to lack all feeling of responsibility, and are no better than moral jellyfish.

A Personal Confession

It is bad for children to be drugged and put to sleep with moral soothing syrup. They take the sweet opiates until they come to the point where they feel no pain nor unrest from having done wrong, and then they are morally drowsy through all those formative years. It is still worse when men and women carry this baby habit up into maturity. When asked why he is not a Christian, some man, looking around for a convenient place to lay the blame, will tell you he was made to go to church too much when he was a boy; or that he was taught a stern and rigorous theology which repelled him. It is a mean, false excuse. It is an ugly piece of cowardice when a man slanders the honest efforts of his Christian parents to make a good man of him, rather than shoulder the blame of his failure to serve God. The people who tell you that they are kept out of the Kingdom by the inconsistencies of Christians; and those who plead that they are not good enough to begin to do the will of God; and those who say that there are things about religion they do not understand, as if they imagined, for a moment, that the rest of us had solved all mysteries—these friends are all hiding behind the door to avoid the direct responsibility of walking through it. They are not ready to say, "I have sinned," and to ask for a place where they can humbly serve the Father.

There are people in every community who have no moral life at all. Not that they are entirely immoral, but they make their decisions touching conduct from habit, from convention, from the chance impulse or mood, rather than from a direct sense of obligation to a moral law. And in accounting for their characters, they have the same defective sense of personal life. "Circumstances over which they had no control" made them as they are. They leave out their own personal agency, as Aaron did when he excused himself to Moses by saying that the people gave him the gold, and "then I cast it into the fire

A Personal Confession

and there came out this calf." He does not deny the wickedness of making idols, but he would insinuate that "the fire" was to blame. He cast in the gold and somehow "there came out" that image of a calf that would so readily appeal to the ignorant Israelites, fresh from the sight of the worship of the sacred bulls in the land of Egypt.

Circumstances, environment, the world, these are the fires, as Phillips Brooks says, into which men cast their natures, and then the blame for the worldly, or unbelieving, or insincere men that result, is laid upon the dumb furnace. The current is setting in a certain direction; men put their boats into it and drift; and then they excuse themselves from further responsibility by claiming "the current did it." This would-be helplessness and laziness so confuse the moral vision and so debilitate the nature that at last the man is not a man but a thing. How healthful and hopeful in the midst of all this fog is the clear, definite acknowledgment of the prodigal—"I have sinned!" It brought him, as it will bring any man, into the presence and the favor of his father.

In these hard times, we hear much about the great industrial régime and the commercial system that holds us all. Many of us are believers in the sociological side of religion; we are waiting for the consolation of industrial Israel, and trust that we shall not die before we have seen the Son of Man coming in that part of His Kingdom. But a great deal of the trouble has resulted from our own wrongdoing. The liquor bill of the United States last year was $962,000,000, and the tobacco bill was $600,000,000 more. Those are not necessities—they would be termed luxuries; and in many cases have proved themselves most hurtful luxuries. The larger part of the nine hundred and sixty-two millions of money for rum came from the workingmen, the poorer men. Before we lay the entire blame of the hard times upon a Republican

A Personal Confession

or upon a Democratic administration; before we talk ourselves hoarse as to the evils of a competitive or the blessings of a cooperative system, we had best take heed to our own ways. We have built huge breweries and distilleries; we have spotted our cities all over with rum shops, and the well-being of our country has suffered in consequence. Nine hundred and sixty-two millions of dollars poured down the throats of men to their own hurt in a single year would have put bread enough and to spare in many a father's house. Industrial reformers sometimes sneer at such observations as being mere preaching, and not economic wisdom. But they point to a lesson that must be learned. If a workingman spends a third or a tenth of his narrow income for rum, he will have just that much less to spend on objects that make life worth living, whether he happens to be under a Democratic or a Republican administration, a competitive or a socialistic régime. Men have sinned against the law of well-being and in the sight of God, and that wrongdoing must be admitted and corrected before they can come in to the feast and begin to be merry.

We hear much in these days about social Christianity. There is "a gospel for the state, a gospel for the city, a gospel for industry, and a gospel for society." All these concrete relationships existing among men need to be transformed by the renewing of their minds. The whole face of organized life should shine with new light, and its institutional garments should become white and radiant. But there is danger, meanwhile, lest the gospel of the individual be obscured, and lest we come into bondage to a false way of thinking. There is no society, or state, existing as such—the only realities are the individual lives composing these organizations and grouped together under convenient names. Corporate life can only repent and believe the gospel of its renovation, as the individuals concerned come to have the mind and

A Personal Confession

spirit of Christ. Selfish men will inevitably maintain a selfish industrial system, and we shall never be able to make a perfect social order until we have perfect men to serve as material. And surely the only agency that will furnish us the sort of individuals requisite for that ideal society is the omnipotent grace of Almighty God, appropriated by repentant, confessing, and believing men. I am not saying this because it is the orthodox and fitting thing for a clergyman to say, but because the fatal criticism upon most of the social and industrial schemes proposed, is that we have not enough of good character on hand to work them. The quantity of reliable character demanded will come as men recognize their sins, confess them, and obtain such forgiveness and grace as will enable them to live changed lives.

When we come to deal with the evils and misfortunes of a world that is out of joint, we must be ready to see and confess our personal participation in causing the dis-

Two Parables

order. The capital *I* must not be merged in misty talk about humanity. Each man must draw a clear line around his own agency in the matter, and if he has sinned and done evil in the sight of the order that should have obtained, he must say so. If we are square and honest, we cannot escape the need of personal acknowledgment of guilt. You could have done better; you could be living a more useful life now; you could make your daily life at once more nearly an expression of the will of God. No evasion of this fact or of our share of responsibility for the existing condition will be atoned for, by large flourishes about the Gospel of the Kingdom or the regeneration of the corporate life. An ounce of clear, cold honesty is worth a ton of warm, vague sentimentalism, when we seek to put ourselves right with God and man, or to make the world better.

Many are ready to join in general confessions that do not mean anything, nor commit them to any obligation to face about.

A Personal Confession

We have all erred and strayed from the way; we have done things that we ought not to have done, and have left undone things that we ought to have done; we are miserable offenders. Human nature is weak. To err is human. All these pious commonplaces may be very well as general statements in a liturgical service, but to make good character, the confession must become more personal and definite. The most polite and humble reference to the general imperfectness of human life and the faultiness of the world at large, does not take the place of the frank admission, "I have sinned." We are born and we live and we die not collectively, but as individuals; and we are saved and become useful servants of the living God in the same personal way.

The natural attitude of church members is one of personal confession of need. Your neighbors might say that people join the church because they feel they are so good —better, in fact, than their fellows. How queer that sounds! The exact opposite, of course, is the truth. Some candidates for membership came before the church committee last week. What did they say? What did you say when you came? "We are better than the average people—in fact, our lives are about right?" No; they told us they had sinned against heaven and before men; that they desired to make open confession of their need of forgiveness and of a Savior, and to ask for the help and fellowship of the Christian church. When our hearts begin to believe unto righteousness, our mouths also make confession unto salvation. The people who turn their backs on religion are the self-satisfied ones who say they do not need its help. Those who kneel before God in prayer; who reverently open their Bibles to learn the will of God; who assemble at the table of their Lord, that their deepest hunger may be fed, are the ones who, by their whole habit, make the standing confession, we have sinned, and we are asking the mercy and the help of God.

A Personal Confession

It is strange that people have a false sense of shame about confessing that they have sinned and need the saving help of God. The pure air of the New Testament is one of frank confession. You find it on every honest pair of lips, save the lips of our Lord, who knew no sin. At the approach of Christ and upon the revelation of His power, the cry of Peter was, "Depart from me, for I am a sinful man." John said, "If we say we have no sin, we deceive ourselves; but if we confess our sins, He is faithful and just to forgive us." James encourages men to "confess their faults one to another, and to pray for one another that they may be healed." And the greatest apostle, not at the opening of his Christian life, but near its close, writes that "This is a faithful saying and worthy of all acceptation, that Christ Jesus came into the world to save sinners, of whom I am chief." As you walk in company with these men who have been the moral leaders of the world, you become conscious of the essentialness of personal confession.

It is the only honest and healthy basis for the beginning of right life. Men may make for themselves soft cushioned seats out of the excuses they frame; but if they propose to be real men, nothing is so good as the plain, straight-backed chair of absolute honesty. Openly acknowledge the fact that you are a sinful man and need the grace and mercy of God. Take your place among those who have nothing to say of themselves, except that they hunger and thirst after righteousness, and look to God to be filled. Admit that you are in want of better and more abundant life, and arise and go to the Father with your confession that you may receive it. "He that covereth his sins shall not prosper; but whoso confesseth and forsaketh them shall have mercy." To make open confession is to uncover the nature to God and to invite His unhindered approach.

The clear utterance as to the sense of

A Personal Confession

personal lack and need is one that always calls out our human sympathy. The Harvard and Yale men had just rowed a celebrated race. Yale had won, as Yale has a way of doing. At the Harvard boathouse a great company of students were talking with the oarsmen and trying to account for the defeat. One man blamed it on the coach. Another felt that the shell was not built right. John Doe was confident that the stroke had been too long, and Richard Roe was sure it was not long enough. At last one of the Harvard crew spoke out: "I know why we were beaten"—everybody listened—"we did n't row as fast as they did." Every Yale man and every other man would love him for the frank admission that the fault was not in the coach, nor the oars, nor their stars, but in themselves.

Have charity. Have a wide, all-embracing patience and charity — for everybody but yourself. Find excuses, make allowances, temper judgment with mercy in regarding the failings of others; but when you take yourself in hand, get up and sit on the judgment seat and administer counsel in the spirit of clear and definite justice. Unconsciously there will creep in as much constitutional self-pity as will be wholesome for you. Strive to be strict and sternly honest, and where you find yourself at fault, say plainly, "I have sinned." The great forgiving mercy of God will be all the more eager to meet your hard, firm honesty while you are yet a great way off; and instead of the place of a hired servant which you meant to ask in connection with your confession, will bestow upon you the ring and the robe and the kiss that belong to a reinstated son.

The old books of devotion may sound extravagant to us in their statements as to the sense of sinfulness. Some of the hymns we use sound unreal with our present habit of mind; many of the sentences in the "Imitation" are laid aside by the modern reader as obsolete. Perhaps the

A Personal Confession

ascetic view was morbid, but in our day the sense of sin is all too superficial. The feeling that we have broken the law, violated the divine order, disobeyed the will of our Maker, sinned against heaven and in the eyes of men, is faint where it ought to be deep and strong. The easier way of thinking is reflected in our very terminology. Stealing shades off into "kleptomania;" adultery is an "irregular relation;" lying and cheating and other wickedness have all their diminutive titles so that they may be referred to with less offense to the morally sensitive. If we should go on mixing our colors and confusing our judgments until we put darkness for light, and light for darkness; until we call evil good, and good evil, then our moral life would be over, and our alienation from God would be complete.

This parable is, indeed, the classical passage regarding the mercy and helpfulness of God; but remember that it is always to be read in its due order. The father loved his son and longed for his return. He was watching and waiting for that event, so that he caught sight of him instantly even when he was yet a great way off. But he did not carry out the ring, the robe, and the feast, and bestow them upon the prodigal while he was yet with the swine, and wasting himself by living with low companions. The son must leave the far country and must be on his way to his father, with a confession in his heart and on his lips—then, and then only, can he claim the blessing and acceptance of the Father. If we say, by our attitude toward God, that we have no sin that needs repentance and confession for its effacement, we deceive ourselves, and the truth is not in us. "But if we confess our sins, He is faithful and just to forgive us our sins and to cleanse us from all unrighteousness."

The Watchful Interest of the Father

"When he was yet a great way off, his father saw him."

The young man had been what we call rapid. He came into his fortune early in life, which was perilous. Our little boats are not able to carry full sail, and when they go before the wind with all their canvas spread, they are apt to go upon the rocks. In the far country he found that so long as he had plenty of money to spend, he had plenty of friends to help him spend it. Then he found that the money being gone, the false friends were gone, too. He had spent all, and began to be in want, and no man gave unto him. He got down so low that he was feeding swine and earning but a meager living by it. He remembered the wholesome plenty of his father's house. He resolved to go back and begin life over again, even though he had to start as a hired servant. On reaching the vicinity of his former home, he would be ashamed to meet people in the road. But no one knew him; he looked like a tramp, clothes torn, dirty, ragged, shoes worn out—the first thing his father did, you remember, was to call for a robe and shoes. The prodigal would have felt ashamed to have people recognize him, but it was even worse to feel that his wicked life had changed him beyond recognition. At last he saw the old home! There is the figure of a man who has rapidly grown gray during these sad years! But though the eyes were dim, the moment they fell upon that vagrant-like figure, they knew him. The loving eyes of the father did what the indifferent eyes of the neighbors failed to do. When he was yet a great way off, his father saw him and had compassion, and ran and fell on his neck and kissed him. The moment he had kissed him, there began to issue also from his lips words of forgive-

The Watchful Interest of the Father

ness, directions for his comfort, utterances of rejoicing that the son whom he had mourned as "lost" and "dead," was "found" and "alive again."

How did the father chance to see him so soon? He was watching for him. His eyes were on the road where the son who was tired of the want and the husks, the harlots and the swine of the far country, might travel back to his father's house. You remember Lachlan Campbell in the Bonnie Brier Bush. He was the stern old Calvinistic elder, who sat in judgment on the theology of the Glen, and straightened out the minister who slipped in a bit of compassionate heresy that seemed to minimize the awful sovereignty of God. His daughter Flora at last rebelled against the harsh régime of her home, and ran away to London. The Elder was no less severe upon his own; he related her fall at the next meeting of the Session, and with his own lips moved that her name be stricken from the church roll. But afterward he got a glimpse of the New Testament; he had been locked up in the Old. He had always said "Jehovah," but now he learned to say "Our Father." He caused a letter to be written to his erring daughter asking her to come home, and assuring her of forgiveness. Then the stern old man, thinking his daughter would return at night, lighted a huge parlor lamp that was kept for show, and placed it at the window. "And every night till Flora returned, its light shone down the steep path that ascended to her home, like the divine love from the open door of our Father's house."

I want to preach to you this morning about the way the Heavenly Father watches the road by which men slowly and painfully make their way up to nobler living. He recognizes even the faint beginnings and the first awkward efforts at goodness. Even the unsuccessful attempt to resist temptation and the blundering movement toward the right, never fall to the ground without His notice. His clear eye

The Watchful Interest of the Father

pierces through the mistaken theology of men, through their lack of knowledge touching the historical revelations He has made, and gathers into its loving attention the faltering steps of every man who is even faced toward his Father's house. He is the joyful witness of all conduct that by its spirit indicates a potential faith in the saving grace of Jesus Christ. The statement is full of comfort to the prodigal and to this whole imperfect world of ours, that "when he was yet a great way off, his father saw him." We rejoice in the fact that God comes out to meet His children and show them the way and bear them company, when they undertake to live new lives.

Remember the reluctant forgiveness that we sometimes dole out to wrongdoers! Remember how liable we are to question the motives of certain men who are facing about and beginning to show an interest in religion! Remember how slow of heart we are to believe that bad men can actually become good men by the grace of God! Then walk out into the sunshine of a statement like this text. The neighbors might have said, "He was starved unto it; he had spent all, and no man gave unto him." "He has come for the loaves and the fishes, the bread, and the robe, and the shoes of his father's house." "We will wait five years to see if he 'holds out,' and then we will know, for sure, whether or not he is sincere." There was none of this with the father; no questioning as to his purpose; no withholding of forgiveness until a year of good conduct had demonstrated his clearer right to it; no inquiry as to possible mixed motives. Nothing but eager haste to welcome to a father's heart the man who was tired of doing wrong and was ready to do right. When he was yet a great way off the loving, gracious helpfulness of the father met him, to make his further entrance into the new life easier and more joyous.

First let me speak of how the Father's loving recognition reaches us while we are a

The Watchful Interest of the Father

great way off as to the correctness of our belief. It is said, "No matter what a man believes, so long as he is sincere." It is a lazy, false, and misleading statement. A man might be ever so sincere in believing that corrosive sublimate is as wholesome as pure water; if he drank half a pint of it, it would kill him. Some things are wholesome and some are deadly; we must discriminate and govern ourselves accordingly. Some things are true and some are false. A man is under strict obligation to do his best to know the truth, and to believe and to live by the truth for his soul's health. The Scriptures recognize this in their constant effort to lead every man into the presence of that Light in which there is no darkness at all. To this end they boldly assert the pre-eminence and the authority of the revelation made to men through the Hebrew people. Even so broad and catholic a teacher as our Lord said frankly, "We know what we worship, for salvation is of the Jews." And in defining His own position, He said, "I am the way, and the truth, and the life; no man cometh to the Father but by Me."

But along with this claim and this endeavor there is the recognition of the fact that technical correctness of theological theory is not essential to acceptance with God. Men who, in the colloquial sense, are a great way "off," theologically, are seen, and blessed, and used by the Father. Now and then the Scriptures draw back the curtain and we look out beyond the borders of the Hebrew people and see men in the distance controlled by the Spirit of God, and speaking the truth of God. The narrow minds of our own day have sometimes denied the existence of divine inspiration outside the chosen people, but the Scriptures acknowledge it and utilize it as a part of the body of spiritual instruction given to mankind. Balaam was a pagan, living somewhere beyond the Euphrates, but he held communion with the true God, and is allowed to possess the Spirit of God. The

The Watchful Interest of the Father

whole account of his struggle to serve two masters by making terms with both God and Balak, finds its point in the fact that he was acting in the face of a genuine revelation. He acknowledges the divine compulsion laid upon him. "If Balak would give me his house full of silver and gold, I cannot go beyond the word of the Lord my God, to do less or more." His splendid words, preserved in Micah, are often quoted, as giving us the very gist of religion. When Balak came to consult him, with the rewards of divination in his hand, Balaam answered: "Wherewith shall I come before the Lord? Shall I come before Him with burnt offerings? Will the Lord be pleased with thousands of rams or with ten thousand rivers of oil?" That might have been the reply of formal superstition; it might have been the answer of undue trust in the legal system of ceremonial requirements. But with a clear insight as to the essentials of religion, he replies: "He hath shewed thee, O man, what is good; and what doth the Lord require of thee, but to do justly, and to love mercy, and to walk humbly with thy God?" This from a pagan who lived when the children of Israel were wandering in the wilderness, when the Holy Land was still in the hands of the Canaanites, and when only the faint beginnings of this holy Book had been committed to writing! Truly, when he was yet a great way off his Father saw him and inspired him, and used him for the moral instruction of his people.

The Book of Job entered through the same wide, hospitable door into the body of holy writ. The discussion of divine government and of the problem of human suffering is carried on there by pagans with an Arab sheik in the land of Uz. They do not quote nor appeal to the Hebrew Scriptures then in existence. They simply bring their moral reason to bear on the hard question before them, and the whole movement of their contention is outside the pale of Hebrew revelation. Yet the Spirit of

The Watchful Interest of the Father

God breathes from these pages, and this book rightly holds an honored place in the sacred canon.

The same thing is seen when Cornelius, a Roman who had not renounced his heathenism, but who was a man of reverence and charity, came to Peter. It required a heavenly vision to prepare Peter for the interview and to make him sufficiently broad church to admit this uncircumcised Gentile into the fold of God's acceptance. But after "Peter thought on the vision," he heartily welcomes this choice plant of righteousness, although it grew outside the garden of the Hebrew religion. "Cornelius, thy prayer is heard and thine alms are had in remembrance in the sight of God. . . . . Of a truth I perceive that God is no respecter of persons; but in every nation he that feareth Him and worketh righteousness is accepted of Him."

The same Spirit spoke through Paul when he stood on Mars Hill and faced the heathen idolaters of Athens. Pointing to their altar inscribed, "To the Unknown God," he cried: "Whom ye ignorantly worship, Him I declare unto you. He is not far from any one of us, for in Him we live and move and have our being; as certain of your own poets have said, ... we are also His offspring." In every case there is recognition of the fact that the Father sees men who are a great way off from the main current of divine revelation, and that He helps them to know more of that truth which should one day make them free.

Let me appeal to a still higher authority. In the scene of the last judgment portrayed by our Lord Himself, certain men are held to be good enough to have these words pronounced upon them: "Come, ye blessed of my Father, inherit the Kingdom prepared for you from the foundation of the world." The Son of Man, representing humanity, says to them, "I was hungry, and ye gave Me meat." It startles them.

The Watchful Interest of the Father

They do not seem to have known Christ, nor to have suspected the relation of the kindly activity, in which they had been engaged, to the Lord of life. "Lord, when saw we Thee hungry?" They had simply obeyed that universal principle of duty which bids us help the needy, and, in doing that, they had unwittingly, it seems, been brought into vital and saving relations with the Redeemer of the world. Think of what that passage suggests! The Son of Man upon the throne of His glory, and before Him gathered all nations! Among those nations are some who are such strangers to the trend and drift of Christian thought that they do not know the intimate connection between serving the needy and serving Christ. Yet, though they are a great way off in their knowledge of Christian revelation, the Son of Man sees them and welcomes them: "Come, ye blessed of My Father, inherit the Kingdom."

Those who would limit the work of

Christ to the days of His earthly activity, and to the circle of those who have subsequently been put in possession of the Christian documents, deny the force of such passages as these, and they dishonor the Lamb of God, whose eternal office it is to take away the sins of the world. God has not been speaking with His Hebrew children "face to face as a man speaketh with his friend," and leaving all His other children in blank silence. The pre-eminence of the Hebrew knowledge of morality and religion comes from the fact that they were peculiarly sensitive and responsive on spiritual lines. The Hebrew nation became the chosen people because, somehow in the general division, to it was given five religious talents, while other nations were less generously endowed. But God hath not left Himself without witness anywhere, nor has He created any men totally lacking in ability to respond to that witness. Whatever moral light has fallen on the page of life in China, or in India, or in darkest

The Watchful Interest of the Father

Africa, has come from the true light that lighteth every man that cometh into the world. We can rejoice to believe that even though such men, in their knowledge of religion and in their ability to receive moral truth, were a great way off, yet the Father has seen them, and has hurried to meet every sincere movement toward right living, that He might lead it into His own house and acquaint it with the grace and truth that comes by Jesus Christ.

One day Jesus was walking in the midst of a crowd that pressed upon Him from every side. Suddenly He exclaimed, "Who touched Me?" The disciples were almost amused at the query. "Master, the multitude throng Thee and press Thee, and askest Thou, Who touched Me?" But the believing, appealing touch of that suffering woman could not be hid by the mass of careless contact. She had been ill for twelve years, and could not be healed by her physicians. She said, "If I may touch but His clothes, I shall be whole." It was

Two Parables

a blind, unreasoning sort of faith. It was akin to the superstitious reverence of the Roman Catholic for relics, for the bones of saints, for the holy coat of Treves. This woman looked for her help to the hem of the genuine holy coat. But though she was a great way off in attributing efficacy to the clothes and in imagining she could stealthily secure her health and shrink away with it in the crowd, Christ saw her appeal and blessed it. And when she came and fell down at His feet confessing her strange trust, He added another blessing: "Daughter, be of good comfort; thy faith hath made thee whole; go in peace."

In the second place, the Father sees us when we are a great way off in our moral attainments. Those who fancy that God takes little personal interest in men until they are well established in saintliness need to read this parable again. He sees men trudging along who have only started for home. He sees them when they are just turning away from the old life, and making

The Watchful Interest of the Father

bold to say, "I will arise and go to my Father." He looks even beyond that; He recognizes the unfulfilled purpose of the heart. When David cherished a desire to build a temple in honor of the God who had given him victory over his enemies and established him firmly upon the throne, he was not allowed to carry out his wish because of his wars. And his disappointment is broken to him by those divine words of gentleness, "Thou shalt not build the house; nevertheless thou didst well, that it was in thine heart." It is not simply what men have done or have ability to do now, but what they have the genuine desire to do. The loving purpose is seen and acknowledged, even though it is a great way from its fulfillment.

In certain lodge rooms you have seen a great eye painted on the ceiling. Wherever you stand in the room it looks directly at you. It turns all ways like the flaming sword that kept the garden of the Lord. It serves to remind the members of the fraternity, that as all their movements in the lodge room are within the immediate attention of that eye, so all their actions in daily life are under the all-seeing eye of the Omnipotent God. The fact that God does see us all the time has sometimes frightened children. It becomes to them an almost hateful spying upon their little shortcomings. It ought not to be interpreted solely on the adverse side. "His eye seeth every precious thing," we are told in the Book of Job. The despairing effort at goodness that some better nature makes yonder in the slums, only to fall back and fail under the constant pressure of a hindering heredity and an evil environment; the wistful look at active usefulness that comes from a crippled and broken life; the timid, unconfessed, unbaptized desire to know the Savior of the world, and be at peace with Him, that fills some life, but which is held back by some blindness from open identification with the Kingdom of God; the groping steps of one who walks as yet in

The Watchful Interest of the Father

the twilight, but who is beginning to feel that life must have a deeper and holier meaning—all these things would not pass muster as Christian conduct; they might not be named before the church committee as grounds for admission to membership in the church. But in the sight of the Father they are all "precious things," and He sees them even though the fulfillment toward which they look is yet a great way off.

Ministers constantly wish that more people would attend church, and that more of those who do attend would make open confession of their allegiance to our Lord. Our work in life is to add to the number of professing and practicing Christians. But we should be narrow and mean if we estimated the growth of the Kingdom of God solely by the number of those who unite on profession of faith with our various churches. When I look into quarters where the unchurched, unbaptized activities of life are carried on, I see that God has other sheep which are not of this fold, nor of the Presbyterian fold, nor of the Methodist fold, nor of any denominational fold. There are men who seem, by their actions, to possess the spirit of faith, but who have failed to give it adequate outward expression—them also, I trust that God at last will bring, that there may be one fold and one shepherd.

Railroad men are often spoken of as non-church goers, and are sometimes called an ungodly class of men. Many of them are not seen regularly in the house of God, and many of them, perhaps, not at all. But you rarely hear of an engineer deserting his post in the hour of peril, or flinching from his duty when he sees accident and death on the track ahead. You more often find him buried under his engine, his dead hand still grasping the throttle or the air-brake. We are told, sometimes, that physicians are skeptical, irreligious men. Their studies may incline them to materialism; concentrated attention on the body may obscure the claims of the spirit. Their

The Watchful Interest of the Father

professionl duties often hinder their regular and constant attendance at public worship. But you never heard of a physician, worthy to bear the name, who refused to go and treat a poor sufferer until he had been assured that there would be the financial ability to meet his bill. They place their healing skill at the call of the public, and trust that compensation may come at the end. Much of it never does come. The doctor may or may not drop his dollar in the plate when the charity collection is taken, but no class of men gives more to the poor than do our city physicians. It is well known that with all their knowledge of medicine and hygiene, they die before their time. They are prematurely worn out by exposure and overwork—much of it unpaid work, rendered as a labor of love to those who suffer pain. These two classes of busy men will suffice for illustration. It seems, sometimes, that they show a deficiency on the side of life that we call piety. They might look confused if we were to ask them, "Have you been born again?" "Are you justified by faith?" But these are not the only texts in the Bible. It is good when our eyes fall upon the engineers and the physicians, and the many similar lives, to remember that our Master also said, "Greater love hath no man than this, that a man lay down his life for his friends."

When we visit a cornfield, we can only take into our estimate the corn that is actually up. The swelling, sprouting grains below the surface that have not broken ground lie beyond us. In the great field of human nature, where "He that soweth the good seed is the Son of Man," we feel our limitations when we attempt to estimate the prospects for a great harvest of righteousness. The Christian goodness that has pushed up into sight, spread itself upon the rolls of our churches, entered into benevolent activities, and is uttering its clear and definite testimony, we know. But those hidden germs and seeds of good character, it doth not yet appear what they

The Watchful Interest of the Father

shall be. However, the eye of the Father can recognize and rejoice over these hopeful, fruitful indications, even when their perfect fulfillment is yet a great way off.

Ministers are often asked at what age children should be allowed to unite with the church. No fixed rule can be given; it all depends on the child and on the quality of the home life in which the child is to grow. It is not wise to urge careless and reluctant boys and girls into church membership. But when they grow thoughtful and earnest, when they desire to show their love for the Savior by uniting with the church He founded, it is not good to postpone one of the very ends for which we have been praying. They do not understand the meaning of Christian life as they will later, but even the oldest and ripest Christians are still "disciples." When children have the love of Christ in their hearts, and when they choose His way as their part in life, they are good enough to be enrolled in the school of Christian goodness and to have a place at the Father's table. He sees these innocent beginnings of Christian life, even though judged from an adult standard they are a great way off, and He hastens to give them place within His own substantial recognition.

But let me ask, How does the Father see men and run to them while they are a great way off? It has been said that in this parable, the classical passage on repentance, there is no mention of atonement or of mediation between God and man—the son comes simply and directly to the Father. But the Father saw the son while he was a great way off, because He had been looking for him; He had been going down to the gate and straining His eyes to get the first glimpse of a possible return. And when you state this attitude and disposition on the part of God, what have you done but to describe the revelation He made of Himself when "the Son of Man came to seek and to save that which was lost?" This watchful, eager, loving interest of God in

The Watchful Interest of the Father

men who are afar off is but another name for the grace and truth that came by Jesus Christ.

I preach this to you as the Gospel of the Son of God. We have all done wrong. We are all under obligation to live holy lives. But we are not left to find our way up to complete righteousness, unaided. We are not called upon to establish ourselves in holiness before there can come a look of recognition from the source of all goodness. Our redemption is undertaken from above. It is a part of the whole system of things in which we live. The Lamb was slain from the foundation of the world; and without that redemptive purpose of Him who was in the beginning with God, was not anything made that was made. The whole movement for our moral welfare was inaugurated and is sustained by the omnipotent hands of Him whose watchful, fatherly interest I have preached to you this morning. If we ever learn to love God, it will be because He first loved

Two Parables

us. If we become saints, it will be because while we were yet sinners Christ died for us. If we find our way at last into our Father's house to go no more out, it will result from the fact that while we were yet a great way off He saw us and hastened to offer us His own abundant helpfulness.

PRINTED BY R. R. DONNELLEY
AND SONS COMPANY AT THE
LAKESIDE PRESS, CHICAGO, ILL.

www.ingramcontent.com/pod-product-compliance
Lightning Source LLC
Chambersburg PA
CBHW020802230426
43666CB00007B/813